THE STRENGTH OF YOUR STRANDS

The Journey to Loving Your Natural Hair

JOSHICA KIAH CRAIG

Copyright 2021 © by Big Light Publishing

Published by Big Light Publishing
Front Cover Design: Joshica Kiah Craig
Editor & Cover Photo: Dominique Dejon Craig

Uploading or distributing photos, scans and any content from this book without prior permission is theft of the author's intellectual property. Please honor the author's work as you would your own. Thank you in advance for respecting our author's rights.

For permission requests, please contact the publisher at: hello@thestrengthofyourstrands.com

The Strength of Your Strands, The Journey To Loving Your Natural Hair

www.thestrengthofyourstrands.com
Instagram @thestrengthofyourstrands
Facebook @thestrenghtofyourstrands

ISBN 978-0-578-88170-6

Printed in the United States of America

*For every black girl who aspires to live life unapologetically.
To every black woman who's ready to unleash her power.*

TABLE OF CONTENTS

Introduction 1

Your Roots 3
   Chapter 1 – Happy to be "Nappy" 5
   Chapter 2 – Who Told You Your Hair Was Not Beautiful? 9
   Chapter 3 – The History of Black Hair 17
   Chapter 4 – Creamy Crack 21
   Chapter 5 – The Miseducation of Madam C. J. Walker 25

Your Strands 29
   Chapter 6 – What Does Your Hair Say About You? 31
   Chapter 7 – Just Say "No" to That Weave 37
   Chapter 8 – Hair Story 49
   Chapter 9 – I Am Not My Hair 53
   Chapter 10 – It's A- Shame 59
   Chapter 11 – Natural Hair is Professional 65
   Chapter 12 – You're Walking Around Without Your Crown 71

Your Strength 77
   Chapter 13 – Natural Hair Revolution 79
   Chapter 14 – Returning Natural 87
   Chapter 15 – Free Your Mind and Your Hair Will Follow 91
   Chapter 16 – The Bold and the Beautiful 95
   Chapter 17 – Knowing Your Self-Worth 101
   Chapter 18 – Take Up Space 111
   Chapter 19 – The Strength of Your Strands 115

References 125

INTRODUCTION

It took me thirty years to realize that my natural hair was beautiful, after growing up and being repeatedly told that it was not. I lived my life wearing my hair straight and hiding under hair wigs and weaves. It was a defining moment in my life when I finally got it. The change happened after my husband told me my hair was beautiful. After all those years of self-doubt, all I needed was someone to tell me with conviction how beautiful my hair was. I realized that millions of women had probably lived their entire lives without someone telling them that their hair was beautiful, so that is what I'm here to do – to tell you that your hair is beautiful. I'm not here for making excuses about why black women should wear wigs or weaves or have chemically straightened hair. I'm not apologizing for my disdain toward wigs and hair weaves and straight hair. If you're looking for someone who's going to apologize and make excuses for you wearing fake hair and chemically straightened hair, this is not the book to read. If you're looking for someone to tell you to "do you" and wear your hair however you like, this is not the book to read. This book is to free you from anything that is not authentic to you and the degradation of your self-esteem. This book is for helping you rediscover your natural beauty and learn to embrace yourself just as you are. This book is about keeping it real and learning to love the things that you were born with. It's about learning, empowering, and inspiring you to be your best self. This book is about you waking up from the bonds of society and living your full potential. Black hair has been attacked and viewed as an object of disrespect for far too long and it's time to reclaim your superpower and learn to walk confidently in your skin. So, if you're struggling with wearing your natural hair and you choose fake hair or straight hairstyles, then keep reading as I share my natural hair rollercoaster – a series of highs and lows to self-discovery and why it's time for you to step out, own your space, and take back your power.

Part One
YOUR ROOTS

1

HAPPY TO BE "NAPPY"

It was Christmas morning when my family gathered at my Grandma and Grandpa Johnson's home to spread the holiday cheer and exchange gifts. This was one of the best days for a five-year-old, and I was excited to open all of the presents under the Christmas tree. Out of all of the presents under the tree, I was overjoyed to find that my mother had bought me a brand-new barbie doll. I thought that this was the best toy I could have ever received, and I was filled with happiness as I began to play with my doll for the rest of the day. I later discovered that there was one problem with this doll, according to my aunt Della Reese (who was named after the famous actress and singer Della Reese). Aunt Della was the pro-black, dashiki-wearing, back-to-Africa type, and she explained to my mother, (also known as Mommie Dearest, from the movie *Mommie Dearest* – she didn't play) that she should not have bought me that doll because it was white. They went on to argue as to why my mother needed to buy me black dolls. Aunt Della suggested that I needed to see black images like myself so that

I could identify with beautiful black dolls and black women. She shared how important it was for young black girls to see more positive images of women that looked like them. Mommie Dearest, on the other hand, believed that it was not that deep, that it was just a doll, that it didn't matter what the doll looked like since it was only a toy that was going to end up broken and thrown into the trash a few weeks later. It wasn't until that day that I even noticed the color of my dolls but that didn't stop me from enjoying my brand-new Christmas present. Later that day, I saw a shampoo hair commercial with a beautiful white woman swinging her hair while smiling. I turned to Aunt Della and told her, "When I grow up, I want to be white." Aunt Della sat up in her chair, eyes widened as if in shock. The room grew silent as if in disbelief and it was as if time had stood still. She looked around the room to check if everyone could see what had just happened. She looked over at my mother with an intense look, making sure that Mommie Dearest had heard what I had said. She finally looked back at me and asked, "Why do you say that?" I told her, "I want to be white so that I can have long, pretty hair down my back." She laughed as if relieved to find that my dreams of being white were only superficial and told me that I "have pretty hair" and "It will grow long." She reassured me saying, "You don't want to be white. You can have long pretty hair too." My aunt then turned the television off, realizing that I wanted to be a white woman because I had seen it on the television commercial. Aunt Della had her "I told you so" moment as they continued with their debate as to why it was important for black girls to see positive representations of themselves. I remember my aunt's words encouraging me at the time and I looked forward to growing long beautiful hair that looked exactly like the woman I saw in that hair commercial, but it never happened. Growing up as a black girl in the United States, I struggled with learning to love and appreciate being black and loving my natural hair. With black hair being a disgrace, my older sister, Yvette, and I would get teased at school by other black girls and boys, who called us "nappy-headed." Nappy is the dirty word used to describe the ugliest and most unwanted hair type, where the tight curls are described as "beady beads." My hair was always the butt of a joke or the object of ridicule. Using the word nappy became a part of *my* vocabulary and would be something I would use when I wanted to hurt someone. It was used to tear down and cut like a knife. Everyone knew that being nappy meant you were ugly. Whenever I would be called nappy, I would retort to protect my dignity, "I'm happy to be nappy," but I didn't mean that. Deep down, I was unhappy, and I didn't want anything to do with the big bush that sat on the top of my head. On one front, I was fighting the insults hurled at me by my peers, while on the other front, there was the media's influence which glorified white culture. The media influenced me and misconstrued my perception of what I considered beautiful. I had come to discover that black women all over the world had experienced the same things, such as being picked on because of their hair and wanting to be like the white women they see on television and in the movies. Most black women had a similar story of wanting to be that princess or doll or woman in the magazine and on television, and have been trying all of their lives to live like the beautiful white woman that they adore. This form of self-hate had me wondering…

Where did the hate come from?
Where did the negativity about black women's hair come from?
Who told you that your hair was not beautiful?

Let's get to the root of the matter.

2

WHO TOLD YOU YOUR HAIR WAS NOT BEAUTIFUL?

"The man who does not value himself, cannot value anything or anyone." – Ayn Rand

Black /blak/- dirty, spoiled, reflecting or transmitting little or no light, thoroughly sinister or evil; wicked. Indicative of condemnation or discredit, sad, gloomy, characterized by hostility or angry discontent; having dark skin, hair and eyes; characterized by grim, distorted, or grotesque.

It's just like that scene in the 1992 movie *Malcolm X* by Spike Lee, where Malcolm is in jail and reads the definition of black for the first time, and I've only listed half of it. I recently watched the film and thought to myself that the definition of black would not be the same as it was back then, that the dictionary would have been more politically correct in referring to the word black, but no. The same definition of black that existed in the 1940s still exists today, and why wouldn't it? What we refer to as being black is black, and that won't change. The only thing that has changed, however, is the fact that African American people and our culture have been added to that definition. This made me feel different about this label that was placed on us and what we choose to call ourselves. There is no coincidence, however, that we are labeled black and what we see in the media and cinema is no coincidence either.

Reading American history, I've discovered that everything that we have learned and have been influenced by growing up was designed to make us feel inferior to white society. After reading the definition of black, it made me feel like I was the ugly duckling, the outcast. That I was the center of a bad joke and the whole world was in on it. How could we accept being called black and then say that we were proud? How could we turn something so ugly into something so accepted? When you realize that white society sees you as black, you realize that they don't think much of you, and given the history of slavery and the holocaust of black people in America, you would know that to be true. Some might add that things have changed and that we have come a long way since slavery, but the sad truth is that people's opinions about us have not changed and they still see us as black. It's a delicate subject but it is no secret that there was slavery in America. People are met with the worst kind of torture and degrading acts. Black people in the country have been treated in an inhumane and unjust manner for years and continue to be treated that way. Black people have a lot of learning and healing to do because we have lost ourselves along the way, but it is a beautiful thing to see that it is starting with black women loving their natural selves.

I never looked up the definition of black until that day and I wasn't planning on looking it up until later that day, as I was looking for a speech by Dr. King, and he happened to have stated that we should look up the definition of black. Dr. King is known for his involvement in the civil rights movement of the 1960s and his famous "*I Have a Dream*" speech, which he spoke at The March on Washington; but the speech that I was looking for that day was another speech that Dr. King gave in a discount store parking lot at East 105th Street and St Clair Avenue, Cleveland, Ohio on July 28, 1967, entitled "*Don't let anybody make you feel you are nobody,*" where he spoke about a lot of things that plagued the black community, including self-hate. He encouraged black people to know their self-worth and not let anyone make them feel like they are nobody. He went on to say that we should not be ashamed of our heritage or skin color or hair. He recognized that black people's self-esteem was under attack. He realized that it was difficult for black people to love who they were because we struggled with white supremacy and racism. Black people had to deal with hate from another race while not hating themselves. Being a black woman in the United States, I've undergone so many challenges that have caused me to hate myself to the point where I've called my skin and hair ugly.

When I was growing up, the kids in my neighborhood would tease the dark-skinned kids, calling them "darky" or "blacky" as if having dark skin was a bad thing. For years, men and women looked at black, natural hair as ugly, nappy, and unkempt. Well, we have gotten this idea from white America that viewed black people as animals and inferior to them. In turn, black families have perpetuated the hate that we received from other races and have not learned to love and accept each other. We have not realized our beauty and natural potential. My idea that black natural hair is ugly came from white Americans 'idea of white supremacy in America and all over the world. Physiologically, I was taught to think that everything associated with my life was bad and that everything white was good.

When you understand our history and understand that America has a history of degrading black Americans, you understand that not all white people are on your side. For years, the United States Government has oppressed black men and women, taken away our culture, separated our families, degraded us, and robbed us of our pride. It is all so that they can control us and persuade others that we are sub-human and inferior to them. Over the years, we started to believe that. So, it really shouldn't be of any surprise where our ideas about our hair stem from. Black hair has been at the center of black culture and politics in many instances, and as long as there are racial issues in America, they always will be.

The problem that we as black women face is the struggle to fit in with the rest of the world. Because this is a white male-dominated society, we tend to want to be included in white society. Therefore, we change the way we walk and talk and even our outer appearance, including our hair, to make it more acceptable to the white community. This change forces you to look more conservative, which often lacks self-expression and the characteristics that make you uniquely you. We have been conditioned by the propaganda of white supremacy. We continue to emulate Caucasian beauty instead of our own. After years of degradation and oppression from white America, we have believed the things that have been said about us and now we are saying it to each other.

Our ancestors didn't know any other way of life besides the slave mentality and the segregation that took place thereafter. Therefore, as a result, black men in America tried to look and act like white men and black women worked to resemble white women. As far as hair goes, black men would perm their hair like the women did. Black women also wore wigs, and it was all done to obtain the white standard of beauty. Well, years later, many black men, and especially black women, have not gotten away from trying to obtain the white standard of beauty, but who can blame them? Everywhere you turn, there is a beautiful white woman on the cover of a magazine or in a commercial, film, or television. They are the objects of obsession; they are glamorous, prized possessions, love interests, the ones whom every man wants and the ones whom every woman wants to be. If you look at the magazines, all you see are young, skinny white girls who are remarkably beautiful, sexy, and youthful. Despite the attempt of the fashion and entertainment industries trying to include "plus-size" and curvy women (who are simply regular women) or a token black woman, (which was a fad that came and went), the message of being young, skinny, and white is still being spread. Not to mention that the girls who are in magazines and television are just that, *girls*. Most of the models who are hired for the runway and magazines are sixteen- and seventeen-year-old girls and these are the girls whom the media wants us to strive to look like and desire to be. Not to mention white and mixed raced video vixens that our black men love, the dolls that our little girls adore when they are young, and the superheroes and action figures that our little boys admire. The glorification of white people is in every aspect of our lives.

You would be misled to think that you are in no way influenced by media, music, and television because most of the things we buy and do are based on some advertisement or some outside influence of the media. When I was growing up in the 1990s, the tomboy look was in and my style was influenced by my favorite R&B group TLC. I was wearing baggy pants and tank tops with baseball caps; I was T-Boz and my sister, Yvette, was Left-eye, where Chilli would often be replaced by our cousin Tiffany and several of our friends, depending on what day it was. Fashion and hairstyles are still being influenced by music artists and film stars today. I remember when Rihanna flaunted her bright red cut, the next thing you know, every black woman in America had red hair. Not to mention when Beyonce flaunted her blonde cornrows, black women were in line at the braid shop waiting to sport her latest look. They are performers who are there to sell you something and influence your buying decision in some way. What you may not realize is that most women in the industry are fake in more ways than one, but we want to be just like them. The thing about celebrities is that everyone looks up to them as role models. We envy them, want to live like them, and admire them, not realizing that celebrities have insecurities too and they are faced with a lot more pressure to have a certain appearance. We don't realize that celebrities deal with the same issues as we do and that they have been fed the same rhetoric as we have. They go through depression and deal with identity issues as well and it may be ten times harder for them to be themselves when they have a crew of people telling them how to live. The thing is when you constantly look to these celebrities who are dealing with their issues, you're emulating someone who doesn't have it all together and is still growing. Someone who is still learning about *themselves* and working on self-acceptance as well. You are trying to emulate broken people. Instead of trying to be like the broken people whom you don't know, try being yourself and learning more about who you are.

You say you want to be different, you want to be an individual, and you want to be yourself, but you are just following the masses and the rules set by fashion and entertainment. Images have power, and they say a picture is worth a thousand words. So when you constantly see images of glorified white women, that is what will continue to speak to you and shape your perception of beauty. That is why we need to change the focus and redirect our idea of beauty to the natural, proud black woman.

The reason you feel disdain toward your hair is due to years of self-hate – the weight of the negative stigmas that have been placed on you as a black woman. Looking back, I think Aunt Della was right. I needed to see myself not only in the dolls that I played with but also in the media. The fact of the matter was that the images of white women in the media were so powerful that that was whom I desired to be. Growing up, I had what I thought was high self-esteem because I loved my light brown complexion, my slim figure, and my black culture, but until recently, I never realized that my whole life, I had been trying to be that white woman whom I saw in that commercial.

3

THE HISTORY OF BLACK HAIR

Most black Americans trace their ancestry back to West Africa and women from Africa have been wearing their natural hair and hair dressings to symbolize royalty and status in their tribes. Well, let's tell natural hair's story. It was a sign of pride and a symbol of greatness. Natural hair was a symbol of beauty, fertility, strength, status, and culture. So liberating and empowering, it was the center of conversations. It became not only a part of black people's identity and essence but also the mother of unification.

There was a turning point in African history that plucked her children from their roots, literally and figuratively. Black people who once loved nurtured, and cherished natural hair now found themselves slaves to Europeans. To stake their claims, these slave masters ensured that they stripped black people of the very thing that defined their essence – natural hair. Now slaves were shaved once they arrived in the New World. Can you believe it? Natural hair, the defining mark of their identity and culture, their treasured foundation among them, is being removed.

Upon arrival in the Americas, black people were considered inferior to the white race, making black people think that white people were superior. This attack on natural hair was so strong that the tignon law was passed in states like Louisiana. What did their natural hair do to deserve this, you might ask? Nothing. Natural hair was now embraced by her adopted children in America. Seeing how beautifully these free, colored women shone with natural hair, whites decided to put this law in place to "discipline them" by forcing them to cover their hair and dress down. Yet, natural hair and her daughters could not be outdone. What did they do? They adorned their natural hair like the gem that it was in headwraps. And today, that's where your love of headwraps draws from. After all, it's embedded in your blood as was in your ancestors' fierce protection of natural hair. Natural hair rose to even greater prominence as it was styled to show the paths that would lead to freedom. Yes, black, natural hair was etching itself into American history to continue to tell its story.

Fortunately, slavery ended. Thank God, right? But what happened to natural hair? Despite their strong and protective efforts to show that it was best to maintain natural hair exactly as it was, its children had endured so much during that long and arduous period that they felt it was perhaps better to tame it. Black hair, which helped free so many, was once again under attack. An attack that she wasn't right if you wanted to get ahead and be accepted by whites. Black hair didn't quite belong, and it was prettier, more liked if it was now straightened, properly maintained, tamed, and long. What were its children to do when everything they had ended with slavery (except them being treated like second-class citizens)? So, according to *Glamour*, then came Madam C. J. Walker and others, offering natural hair's children as a way to get along. They said flat iron your head. Blacks found ways to maintain their hair while trying to assimilate into mainstream white society. They straightened natural hair and developed tools like the straitening comb, also known as the hot comb, and hair relaxers, better known as a perm. Natural hair – that in the days gone by had been protectively braided, treated with Chebe, and washed so lovingly on Sundays – had become like its children, relegated to the bottom.

Black natural hair was suppressed like its people but not for long. Their identity had been tied to white America and they needed to break free. They needed to move into their own space and create their own stories. Stories of pride, stories of self-awareness, stories of self-acceptance. The civil rights movement came in strong in the 1960s and natural hair was once more the queen supreme. Like reggae artist Chronixx said, "They never told us that black is beautiful, right?" With a celebration, a new-found appreciation of black culture and consciousness, wearing natural hair as she was, natural, and in an afro was the way to go. Back to where it belonged, natural hair now symbolized pride and resistance. With such a strong stance though, the afro was seen by the mainstream as not just another style but also a sign that the wearer was militant.

While it has since taken on many forms from Jherri's to relaxed hair and sew-ins, natural hair is still the undefeated queen. Yes, her beloved indeed moved on from 'fros to styles that were being promoted in the mainstream, but you still can't deny that our people always knew how to make it their own style using accessories or by simply *dripping all that sauce*. Fast forward to today, madame natural hair's beauty is regaled everywhere from the surge in the natural hair movement with protective styling that will remind you of its African roots or cornrows to braids to big chops with fades. You can't deny that it's being appreciated everywhere with a growing fondness. And of course, it's still facing discrimination, but with the 2019 CROWN Act, it'll reign as the queen that it is. As the act ends racial stereotypes against natural hair, especially in the workplace, it gives hope that black people will not only take glory in their melanin but also feel less inclined to appropriate to those mainstream styles. Who knows, maybe you too will return to the foundations of natural hair.

4

CREAMY CRACK

When I was twelve years old, I begged Mommie Dearest for a perm, also known as a relaxer or creamy crack, because Yvette had just gotten one for her thirteenth birthday. Mommie Dearest was the type of woman who saved on salon visits by purchasing a boxed perm and styling her hair herself. So I would see her now and then, applying that thick heavy cream to her hair and watching it turn into silky smooth tresses. When I was a little girl, my mother took special care to braid and twist my hair and put it in cute little girly bows. Sometimes, we would get it braided with beads on the ends, but I was a pre-teen now and it was time to trade in the bows for a bump-n-curl. I still got teased a lot about my hair even though my mother made sure that it was well kept. It didn't matter how it looked, if it wasn't bone straight, I was at risk of being called *nappy* or *beady-bead*. When I got older, I didn't want the little girl styles, so I would resort to a ponytail. I remember one day I wore a ponytail to school and one of the girls in my class was bragging about how she had just gotten a fresh perm. In an attempt to be funny, being the annoying pre-teen that I was, I went up to her and did what no person should ever do – I roughed up her pretty little ponytail. She then returned the gesture and as I laughed it off, I pulled out my bristle brush to brush my thick puffy ponytail back into place. She replied, "At least I don't need a brush to fix my hair, I can just go like this..." as she proceeded to effortlessly brush her straight tresses back into place with her fingertips. Ever since that day, all I wanted was to get a perm so that I could put it into one simple hairstyle, a ponytail. I didn't want curls, a bob cut, or hair down my back, all I wanted was to slick my hair back into a sleek and smooth ponytail with at least six inches of hair hanging down into a slight curl; the perfect ponytail, that's all I wanted. I wanted to have effortless hair that was worth admiration.

Most, if not all, black women, grow up with the same story when it comes to their hair and hair care. "My hair was so long and natural until my mom permed it." It's something we've all heard before. If you laughed, I know you've either heard the story or told it. Why is it that our moms or guardians decided to perm our hair? I'll tell you a couple of reasons. They either didn't know how to manage natural hair or they wanted to straighten it because they felt like their hair was too nappy. It's an ongoing cycle that it's time to break.

Mommie Dearest was reluctant to give perms to Yvette and me as little girls, because of stories like this. Unlike Aunt Della and many other black mothers, my cousin, who had beautiful long hair, was two years old when Aunt Della decided to give her daughter a perm and as a result, all of her pretty, long hair broke off and fell right out. Therefore, Mommie Dearest was determined to wait until we were old enough to get a perm. Little did my mother know, it didn't matter what age we were, those chemicals were strong enough to make a grown man cry. Also, all the stress and strain on the hair, only cause your hair to get dry and brittle and then break off, leaving some with alopecia, scalp burns, and chronic shedding.

After hours of begging, I finally persuaded my mother to give me a perm. She sat me down as she scraped out the leftover bit of perm that was left from her perm kit and applied it to my roots. There was a chill from the cool sensation of the initial application and from the excitement I felt as I got up to look in the mirror. I could hardly wait to see the results as I started to feel my scalp tingle. Mommie Dearest kept asking me if it was tingling and I would tell her "no" only because I wanted to make sure that the perm took to my hair. Mommie Dearest washed out the perm and I was overjoyed to find that my hair was silky and fine. Fortunately, it did not fall out, but, unfortunately, I traded my beautiful thick and full curly locks for thin, damaged stringy hair, all because of the pressure of getting a perm from my peers and getting teased at school.

If you were born in the 1980s like me, you missed the whole 1960s and 1970s, *I'm Black and I'm Proud, Black Power and Black is Beautiful Movement* when getting a perm or a press-n-curl was in. Many black women share the same story of wanting a perm because they wanted to fit in or feel more attractive. Some may not have even had that choice because their mother chose to perm their hair when they were still a child, yet the premise remains the same, we all were trying to achieve the European beauty standard.

Fast forward to when I became an adult, I would avoid going natural and would make excuses as to why it wasn't for me. I would say it was harder to maintain, it was unprofessional, a weave was easier to maintain, or it was just not for me. All of these excuses were simply reasons why I didn't like myself and why I would rather look like someone else. I was ultimately saying that I didn't love myself and I was lost. What I was saying was that I was afraid of wearing my natural hair because I thought it was *bad hair*. I didn't want to go natural because I didn't think much of myself and my self-worth was tainted. I didn't know who I was and I didn't want to learn about myself. I was comfortable being someone else, imitating someone else, hiding behind the mask of fake hair and a false identity.

I was afraid of what people would say or how they would treat me because showing my natural hair might look unbecoming. I was okay with following the crowd and was too afraid to be independent or stand out. I was comfortable letting someone tell me what was attractive and how I should look. I also didn't want to assert my blackness by wearing my natural hair or to even be seen as a sign of rebellion against white, racist society and I was afraid to be unapologetically black.

But I wasn't alone.

5

THE MISEDUCATION OF MADAM C. J. WALKER

When I was growing up, if I had the support of the natural hair community that exists today, I would have grown up loving my natural hair and I would have been a different person. As I got older, Mommie Dearest didn't know how to take care of my natural hair and neither did my grandmother. The only thing my grandmother knew how to do was press my hair to make it straight. I wish I had Mommie Dearest telling me how to take care of my hair as a teenager and reassuring me that my natural hair was beautiful, but that was something that I had to learn on my own. That is something that most black women are learning.

Let's take a look at Madam C. J. Walker. Madam C. J. Walker was born in 1867 in Delta, Louisiana. She was born during the post-slavery, Jim Crow segregation era, at a time when black people were marginalized by being denied the right to vote, hold jobs, get an education, etc. Those who attempted to defy Jim Crow laws often faced arrest, fines, jail sentences, violence, and death. Therefore, black people in America wanted to assimilate with white people, which meant changing their appearance to fit in and appear less intimidating to the white race. Our big afro hair distinguished us from white people and was considered intimidating to white people. Therefore, Madam C. J. Walker experimented with straightening combs and toxic chemicals that were so strong, that they could cause chemical burns on the scalp while uncoiling the tightly curled hair most black people possessed. She began making hair products after experiencing her own hair loss. Her products were displayed as the "cleanliness and loveliness" of African Americans. Black men and women were desperate to look like white people in America, so they bought them. They saw their kinky-curly texture as a problem and Madam C. J. Walker was able to supply the answer. The perm was a popular product used by men and women faithfully. Though Madam Walker created products for natural hair, like her Wonderful Hair Grower pomade, most of her products were centered around changing the appearance of how natural hair looked. The ads she portrayed made it appear that if black women wore their hair straight, they would be more presentable and likely to succeed. Instead of creating products that made natural hair more manageable or made curl patterns pop or that made natural hair shine, Madam Walker created a chemical that damaged natural hair.

THE STRENGTH OF YOUR STRANDS

Many black women consider Madam C. J. Walker to be an icon. We look up to her because she is the first female self-made millionaire, and she was a black woman. She would be a role model for black women if they are entrepreneurs or are seeking to grow their businesses. Madam C. J. Walker was a great and smart businesswoman, but how exactly did she make her money and what exactly was she selling? Just like the hair care industry today, Madam C. J. Walker made millions off of black people's insecurities. I commend her for her business endeavors and the example that she set for black women everywhere but we no longer have to assimilate and change our appearance to fit in. It's hard to write about black women starting at the natural hair movement without talking about why we needed a movement in the first place. It's time now to take her example and refocus it on something that empowers us to not only make money but also love ourselves. Most of our families are still trying to assimilate like the people in the 1800s. We don't realize that the same ideals that we had about our natural hair have been perpetuated throughout history. The things that we have been taught by the members of our family may have had a negative influence on how we view ourselves. There has been miseducation not only of our historical icons, but also of our mothers, aunts, and grandmothers. When I told Aunt Della that I wanted to be a white girl, she offered words of encouragement to uplift me and empower me so that I would feel proud of my brown skin and my kinky-curly hair, but it was hard for me to believe her because unfortunately, despite her pro-black persona, she wore her hair straight. That was the perfect moment to build my little self-esteem and to reassure me that what I had to offer the world was just as great and that I was beautiful with my natural hair even if it didn't grow long, but how could I take a compliment from someone who wasn't representing that? So I spent most of my life trying to achieve what that beautiful white woman in the commercial had – long, straight hair.

When have you been told that your hair is not beautiful?

_____

_____

When have you been told that your hair is beautiful?

_____

_____

How do you feel about your natural hair?

_____

_____

PART TWO

YOUR STRANDS

6

WHAT DOES YOUR HAIR SAY ABOUT YOU?

When you wear hair weaves, wigs, or straighten your hair with relaxers or texturizes, you are saying that you are not comfortable in your skin and that you are not proud of being black. You are saying to yourself that you would rather be white or have white hair. You are saying that you do not care about your *real* hair and would rather get rid of it. You are saying that if you had the choice you would prefer that it grew straight and not curly. It's sad to see that black women make all kinds of excuses as to why we don't want to take care of our natural hair, claiming that it takes too long to style, it's hard to comb, it doesn't look good, it's too dry, it's too thick, when what you are saying is that you're lazy, you don't want to invest time into your hair, you don't like your hair enough to learn about it, you don't like the way your hair looks, you don't want to deal with yourself and you would rather cover it up, straighten it, and forget about it altogether. There is nothing more unattractive than a woman with low self-esteem. Everyone can sense when you don't have confidence in yourself. When you wear a hair weave, a wig, or straight hair, you are saying to the world that you don't love yourself enough to wear your hair. Every time you put on a hair weave or get a perm, it chips away at your self-esteem. You are telling yourself that you are not complete without your wig or hair weave, that you are not whole without putting an Indian woman's straight hair in your head to cover up the hair that you own. You prefer someone else over yourself.

Start putting yourself first. Choose your hair instead. You have been influenced to think a certain way and you will follow the masses just because it's trendy. Start thinking for yourself, and ignore anything that does not serve you. When you are constantly being told that you are not good enough, it's not serving you. When you are being told that you need to change your natural hair, it's not serving you. When someone is telling you that you are not beautiful the way you were born, it's not serving you. It's tearing you down. The hair weave industry is not serving you. It's an attack on your self-esteem. It was not invited to the table but decided to crash the party. Your hair is a part of you, and how you choose to wear it shows how you feel about yourself and where you are in life. Women who wear their natural hair think highly of themselves and don't care too much about what people say about them. They are secure in themselves and are not afraid to be the person they were created to be. They don't hide behind a mask of a hair weave and flaunt it like it's their own. Natural women flaunt what they have and are happy with themselves. You might make excuses as to why you wear fake hair and yet say that you love yourself, but actions speak louder than words. Maybe you're reading this and think, "How dare she say I don't love myself? Of course, I love myself. I spend hours taking care of my hair. I get my hair done, my nails done, and my face is always beat. I slay all day and I'm a strong black woman who has it all together." Well, choosing to wear your hair in a style that is not natural and choosing to manipulate it into something that is widely accepted as a form of self-hate. Self-hate is something that black people have had to face for centuries, simply because of years of trying to assimilate into a racist society and because of what we've been taught to think about ourselves. We have been taught that the darker the skin, the uglier and the more sinister you are. We have been taught the thicker the hair the less sophisticated and the less attractive. I challenge you to take out that weave or that wig and stop wearing straight hair and we'll see how much you love yourself. Take off everything fake and now tell me how much you love yourself. If you find it difficult to do that, then there's a problem. It's easy to be fake and talk about how beautiful and well put together you are when everything about you is manufactured. There's no use trying to defend everything fake about you. It's time to get real and love yourself. If you are constantly thinking negatively about your hair, it's going to show, despite you trying to press it, perm it, or cover it with a wig or weave. What you are saying to yourself and others is that you're not happy with your natural appearance, so you're going to change.

You're hiding and constantly putting out negative energy about yourself. You are saying that you don't know who you are, so you would rather follow the majority of society to look like someone else in an attempt to find yourself. You are saying that your hair doesn't deserve the love and attention that you give to your fake hair and you would rather pay hundreds of dollars to change your appearance instead of taking time to care for your hair and invest in yourself. You have to first be yourself and walk in your truth and start to uplift your true self, not what others are comfortable with or what you feel you should represent, even if it means going against the masses. You have to set your own standards and trends and show the rest of the world what a real black woman looks like. It might not be easy to convince yourself that wearing a hair weave is not authentic and it will be hard for a lot of black women to break free from that image of beauty. Black women are claiming to be unapologetically black but are constantly apologizing for the way they look. You pretend to think highly of yourself and feel that you are secure in yourself because you have a silky weave, but don't have that confidence when the wig comes off. You constantly praise the thing that makes you fit in and looks more white. How can you be sure of yourself *and* be inauthentic? You may even be trying to emulate other black women whom you see and that may be all you know. You might think that there is nothing wrong with this because that person is setting a fine example and they are representing something positive despite their hairstyle. But if they spent hours altering the one thing that characterizes them as black, it doesn't set an example of black pride at all. It's like someone

THE STRENGTH OF YOUR STRANDS

bleaching their skin to be lighter or getting plastic surgery to tone their nose or alter their lips because they think they are too full. Someone who goes to the extent of getting surgery to change their facial features did not like the way they looked and decided to change it. It's the same with your hair. Change your hair and your self-esteem suffers. If you're like me, you may have never really thought about wearing weaves and wigs and straightening hair as hiding or being ashamed of yourself, but now is the time to make the transformation and to start living the life that you were meant to live, being the woman that you were meant to be. When you wear your natural hair, you are saying that you are proud and that you love yourself. You are saying that you are confident and know your value. You are saying that you are bold and strong. You are saying that you refuse to be influenced by the media and other women who tell you how to look and what the standard of beauty is. You are rewriting the rules and setting your own standards. You are saying that you are free to be yourself. You are saying that you are beautiful and that there is nothing to be ashamed of. You are saying, "I'm black and I'm proud." It starts with being confident in your skin, ignoring the stigmas, and knowing the truth about your hair; it's beautiful, and it's your strength. Wearing your natural hair is a statement. It signifies power, beauty, dignity, and confidence beyond measure. Your hair speaks volumes.

7

JUST SAY "NO" TO THAT WEAVE

Black women, you are in trouble! And here's why. Let's take a look at the media and what it is. Advertisements try to sell you cosmetics, clothes, jewelry, cars, etc. These advertisements tell you that your life is not good enough, you are not pretty enough, and you are not skinny enough, so you must buy their products so that you too can look like the sixteen-year-old girl on the Internet. The media is like the big bully that constantly tells you that you're fat and ugly and nobody loves you. Again, the truth about words and ideas is that if you hear them being said to you long enough, you start to believe them. The media is not the only one to blame for your thoughts about your hair, it's also the big beauty industry. The beauty industry is valued at $532 billion and is on an upward trajectory. When it comes to the beauty industry, black women are the number one consumers of hair and makeup products in the United States, spending $6 billion on hair care products alone. Black women spend 85 percent more on hair and beauty aids than the general market. Let's dive deeper into the hair weave industry. You don't love yourself- here's a weave. If you think your hair is ugly – here's a relaxer. You think you look too black – here's a wig. It is an 8-billion-dollar industry centered around your low self-esteem. The hair weave industry is dominated by Asian countries like India and Malaysia, which give black beauty supply stores no chance to buy into yet have no problem selling to. Chris Rock exposed the industry in his documentary, *Good Hair,* and black women everywhere were in an uproar. Black women felt exposed, but not because of this vicious industry because we didn't want to face the truth about their copious spending on fake hair and the use of chemical relaxers. We felt so betrayed by this as if the secret wasn't out and the whole world didn't know that we were wearing weaves and hated ourselves, so much so that we would go broke spending on hair care and chemicals that could burn holes through our skin, all to look white. No one was protesting the weaving industry for exploiting the women of India for their hair, which they were led to believe was being sacrificed for a good cause. Not to mention it's an industry that would never let black beauty supply stores get a piece of the pie. We were embarrassed and upset as if we had some allegiance to our hair weaves. We were hurt because the whole world now knew that we have low self-esteem and would do just about anything to our hair to look like anything other than black. Maybe we were upset because now *we* knew what the rest of the world thought of us. It was not uplifting black women and telling us that we were included and that we were beautiful too. It was telling us that we were excluded and we had to change the way we looked to fit it. To be included in this world, we had to alter our appearance. What do you think that does to your self-image? You believe it if you are constantly trying to change to fit in. An industry that was built on your lack of self-confidence continues to build its empire. This same hair care industry is profiting off of the demise of your self-esteem. The black image is being attacked. Your self-esteem is being attacked. You have to fight for your self-esteem. If you don't first love yourself, no one else will. If you don't appreciate your hair and learn to love and care for it, no one else will. Going natural is more than just a hairstyle, it is accepting who you are, it is fighting for your self-worth and the respect of others. It is a political statement that is telling the beauty industry that you don't care what they think of you or what they think you should look like and you refuse to pay hundreds of dollars and help build their empire to make you feel inadequate. You are saying that this is how you look; it is acceptable and you love it. Lately, there's been a debate that the natural hair movement has gone commercial. Some women wear their natural hair with pride, as a statement that they are unapologetically black. However, some women wear their natural hair because, even though it's not a trend, it's trendy. They don't even wear their afros or a wash-n-go. They do blow-outs, twist-outs, and braid-out styles only to resemble styles that can be achieved with relaxed hair. It's so trendy that natural hair brands have caught the attention of corporate department stores. Big corporations have been buying and selling small natural hair care brands. For many black business owners, that must be a dream come true. However, they don't own much of the market and have to sell to larger conglomerates. Once the business is sold to the highest bidder, they no longer have control over the brand and the image of the company. Therefore, natural hair companies that sold products for black women with afro hair are selling to women with straight, wavy, curly, and all hair types, and it ceases to become a movement for black women to embrace their natural hair, and it becomes a trend. Our lives are not a trend that we can pick up and put down; this is who we are. Other ethnicities can appropriate our culture, but we have to live with what we have. If you're not wearing your natural hair, then you probably use some form of chemicals or wear some form of fake hair. Hair weaves are natural hair's fake friend; even though you might feel like you are doing your natural hair a favor by covering it up, you're neglecting to learn and take care of it, all while lowering your self-worth. While you are considering a weave or wig to be a "protective style", your natural hair is growing limp and frail and how you view yourself is connected to your fake hair, not your own. Now let's talk about "protective styles" or a weave by another name. Once black women started to finally free themselves from the straight-haired, Caucasian image of beauty, here comes the kinky-curly wigs and weaves to once again tear down our self-esteem. Isn't the purpose of going natural wearing your natural hair? Then why is it that we are going back to wearing weaves and wigs? Is it that you don't dare to do the big chop and start over? Is it because the media is taking over once again with the images of women with loose curls in the commercials instead of the thick kinky-curly textures? Is it because your hair still isn't good enough? Every time I look up "protective styles" for braids or cornrows on the Internet, I see women with fake hair and extensions. It's like the weaving industry has found a way to make something authentic to our culture into something that is not even considered attractive unless you add hair. It's like the billion-dollar weave industry has found a way to capitalize on black beauty and culture once again to the point where you don't even see images of black women with their real hair braided and twisted up as if we can't be creative when braiding our hair and create styles that are glamorous or attractive with our hair. Seeing beautiful black women with weaves and wigs and straight hair everywhere I look is disheartening. Every commercial: fake hair. Every film: is fake. At work or on the street corner: fake, fake, fake. I even see black women with fake natural hair. When I see a black woman with fake hair, I think that they are still asleep and not aware of how silly it looks to have fake hair on their head while proclaiming how it's well put together. I just see lost black women with low self-esteem who would rather invest hours of their time and hundreds of their dollars to be something that they are not. Someone who hasn't realized how beautiful they are. You might argue that you just want to change your style and you think it would be fun wearing wigs and weaves and long fake hair, but you don't know why you're wearing it and why you're choosing to have fun with wigs and weaves and not your hair. Our hair is so versatile and fun to explore, yet you resort to wigs and weaves as if your hair cannot look as good or better than straight hair, wigs, and weaves. Once you learn how to care for your hair, then you will see the excitement and the ease in styling your natural locks.

You might be that woman who won't get caught wearing your natural hair, yet you say that you love yourself, not realizing that the reason you are wearing fake hair is the years of self-hate and the degradation of black women. Maybe you're wearing fake hair because you like the low maintenance and have never really thought about how the industry is taking advantage of you. You may not have thought about why you haven't chosen to wear your hair. You may be simply doing what everyone else does and what you feel comfortable with. Well, it's time to stop and think about why you are covering your hair. Ask yourself, are you really afraid to wear your natural hair? Stop and think about why you don't want to wear your natural hair and then ask yourself, what *do* I think about my hair? Then get a pen and a piece of paper and write down all the reasons you cover your hair and why you haven't once decided to go without a hair weave to show your real hair. If you find that you are afraid of what people will say or that you hate your hair or that you think that natural hair is ugly, then it's time to start changing the way you think. Don't be a slave to weaves and wigs. Don't reach a point where you would do anything to hide whom you are by constantly having to change your hairstyle and putting on a front because you disapprove of your appearance. Don't feel the pressure to look like the women in the media to feel loved or liked by others. People love when you are genuine and transparent when you bare it all. Don't feel like you have to live a certain way just to get likes from people you don't even like. It's easy to feel like you're loved on social media and in other aspects of your life, but you're being fake just like those *likes* on social media. Just because you choose not to talk about a problem doesn't mean the problem doesn't exist. There is no way you can heal if you don't address the problem. A lot of natural women are afraid to say it because they don't want to offend or don't want to overstep or maybe they think "To each his own" and "Live and let live." But I'm going to say it for the whole world. Let that hair weave, wig, and creamy crack go! You have been covering your hair for decades and have been trying to change everything that makes you black. By the way, wearing a wig, weave, and straight hair doesn't make you *less* black, even though some women feel it does. If you are wearing your hair straight or covering your natural hair up to fit in or to hide your black culture, then I'm sorry to tell you that people still see you as black. It's okay to be black. It's okay to love yourself. It's okay to wear your natural hair. You can stop hiding. You can stop putting on fake hair or valuing straight styles over your curls. Get back to loving yourself. Get back to being black and proud. I see women posting on social media with hashtags that read: black girl magic, black girls rock, or black is beautiful. I look at the women being represented and I laugh because they are all wearing fake hair. How can you tell other black women that they are uniquely beautiful and awesome when you are not even comfortable being one? Those women are not representing black women. They don't show their natural beauty and yet they praise everything that it means to be a black woman. It's such a contradiction. If you want to spread the message that black women are amazing and beautiful then why don't you be one? A part of them is saying that they are not proud to be black, since everything is fake, and they are trying to hide or change one of the distinguishing factors that makes them a black woman – their hair. How can you tell me that black is beautiful when your appearance says that you are trying to be everything but black? You can start telling yourself that you are beautiful by first showing yourself. You have to set an example for other women and for the women to come because they are watching. You know the saying "Do as I say, not as I do." We may use this phrase because often, we do things that we don't want our children to emulate. The truth of the matter is that children are always looking at what you do and they will end up doing as you do. So, don't be a hypocrite and tell your little girls that black girls rock or your sons that black is beautiful when you don't believe that yourself. If you don't love yourself enough to appreciate the natural hair that grows from your scalp, how do you expect your children to? What will end up happening is the constant perpetuation of the glorification of white beauty resulting in another confused generation that hates themselves too. Your natural self is kinky-curly and there is no reason that you shouldn't be free to be you. Some may not have had the choice between perming their hair and keeping it natural as I did, and some women have never seen their natural hair texture. Our hair is fun to style and when you learn how to define your curls, you too will love the beautiful curl pattern. Everyone else is living out their lives being who they were born to be, yet you are constantly hiding and working to please someone else. You need to show the world that black girls do in fact rock!

THE STRENGTH OF YOUR STRANDS

You would rather spend hundreds of dollars putting someone else's hair on your head or risking your health with chemical straighteners, instead of investing in your hair, and you wonder why you have no edges, why you are losing hair, and why your hair won't grow long. Let that weave go! Start taking care of what you have. Don't spend all your money buying hair and ending up with none of your own. You haven't claimed your power as a woman if you are still hiding and defending something that is not authentic to you, fake hair. Every time you put in a hair weave or wig, you are saying that someone else's hair is better than yours. It's time to start investing in yourself. It's time to start investing in your hair and in taking care of yourself from head to toe. Going to get a hair weave and a wig is not taking care of yourself, because it can damage your hair and your self-esteem. It's time to walk around with the natural crown that our Creator has blessed you with. Don't be ashamed of the thing that makes you special, significant, and unique.

What would happen if you took the time and money you spend on hair weaves and permed styles and invested it in your real hair and yourself – your self-image and your self-esteem? Invest in how you see yourself as a black woman. Hair weaves do nothing for your self-worth except give you a false sense of worth. You constantly get praise and admiration for looking like someone else instead of being who you are. Remove everything that is not authentic to you and start healing. You can't heal if you're still holding on to the things that diminish your faith in yourself. Start putting your energy and focus on your real self. Tell yourself that you are beautiful without hair weaves and straight hair. Every time you tell yourself that "I'm attractive", "I'm beautiful", or that "I rock" when you're weaving a weave or straightening your hair, you're saying that your natural hair is not cool. You are saying that you can't be your best self being real. You are saying that you are your best self when you are fake, and that is false. You are your best self when you are being authentic, inside and out. You can't live your best life while you're hiding. I committed to never return to wearing a wig or hair weave because I'm better than that. I don't want to hide or become a slave to hair weaves. I don't want others to be accustomed to an imitation of myself and not the Joshica I was born to be. I wanted to say to the world and the beauty industry, "No, I'm not going to conform to what you say is acceptable. I'm not going to let you tell me how to live my life while I suffer. I'm not going to let you sell me hair products and fake hair to suppress the pain that I feel inside about my hair and my identity." It was deeper than hair and just like the insults that I heard as a child and adult, it left a mark that needed to be dealt with, and the first step was saying "No" to hair wigs, weaves, and straight hair. You deserve better also. You are better than a hair weave, wig, or hair relaxer. You are better than the person you are pretending to be. Start growing into your own and building your self-esteem by letting go of the wigs, weaves, and perms, and deciding to give yourself a chance. Set yourself free and join the natural hair movement toward self-love, self-care, and natural hair. You can't be the best version of yourself when you're fake. You live your best life when you are free. You live your best life when you are authentic. You live your best life when you live out your truth. That can happen only if you decided to be free to walk around this earth with the things you were born with. Say "no" to that weave and say "yes" to yourself.

8

HAIR STORY

"You can't do your own thing if your own thing is not the right thing." Unknown

I spent years perming my hair along with other girls, and sometimes I would hear them say how they have new growth coming in and it was time for a new perm, even though I thought their hair looked fine. They didn't want even the slightest curl, and would constantly perm their hair to hide any sign of *naps*. As a teenager in high school, I spent years perming my hair with boxed perms and trying to get it bone straight. It worked out just fine for me. My hair looked healthy and shiny and despite the occasional chemical burns on my scalp – that would later heal – I was able to achieve my perfect ponytail every time. After hearing other girls complain about the slightest sign of new growth, I thought maybe that was something I should be concerned about. I thought maybe my hair wasn't straight enough, so after having permed my hair once, I decided I was going to perm it a second time, within a week, only because I saw the slightest sign of texture. Of course, my hair started to break off in the front edges and at the temple, so that was when I decided to return to natural for the first time. I stopped getting boxed perms and finally started to see my texture. My friends would joke that I was on my Erayka Badu, India Arie trip because I was into head wraps and I wore, what I know now to be, heat-damaged curls.

It wasn't until I joined the military that I decided that I was going to perm my hair again and the reason why I decided to perm it instead of keeping it natural was that I didn't know how to take care of my natural hair. I figured it would be easier to get a perm than to try to style my hair or to wear cornrows and look like a boy. Days before I joined the United States Air Force, I slapped some creamy crack in my head and was off to basic training. I kept up with the relaxers for a while until I decided to give my hair a break again. I decided to grow my natural hair out again and discovered the curly texture again and fell in love with it. So during my time in the force, I started growing out my curls. This time, I decided to cut off the relaxed ends to start my natural hair journey again. I went to a new stylist and told her that I wanted to cut the six inches of relaxed ends, hoping that my four inches of natural hair would be poppin'. I was in for a lesson because after she cut off all the relaxer, that four inches of hair turned into a one-inch teeny-weeny afro. I was upset because I thought the stylist had cut off much more than she should have, but once I got home and started playing with my hair I noticed that all four inches were there. That was the first day I discovered shrinkage. I had also gotten my hair professionally dyed at that time. I wanted a honey blonde, but it ended up being a bright amber color, which was against military regulations. So I ended up getting a boxed color treatment and dyed my hair jet black. I later grew fond of my teeny-weeny afro, seeing that it was easy to maintain and my hair looked healthy and flourishing. It wasn't until I started gaining some length that I had issues with my command. I struggled to find ways to style it and ended up just wearing my afro which was getting larger and larger every month. The thing was that my hair started to become a problem when it came to military regulations. At that time, the regulations stated that a woman's hair could not be more than three and a half inches in bulk, and might I add that the hair covers or caps that were a part of our uniform did not help my style in any way, so I started wearing headbands, which was allowed in uniform while leaving my afro to go free. I never had any problems in the military with my natural hair until one day, when during a uniform inspection, my supervisor gave me problems about my headband and wanted me to take it off. But I refused, informing him that the regulations stated that I could wear a headband if it was the same color as my hair (it was a black headband by the way). He was furious and reported me to the command. I, however, was not bothered because I knew what the regulations stated. But my supervisor insisted on giving me a hard time. It wasn't until after the inspection that we settled the matter and I proved to be right. It was after that day that I decided to change my hair again. I figured my hair was becoming a problem and the uniform regulations were making it hard for me to wear my natural hair. That was when I decided to get my hair pressed and curled again, this time into a short pixie cut. And I later began wearing wigs.

9

I AM NOT MY HAIR

It was a cold winter day in New York City, but that didn't put out the spark I had as a young twenty-one-year-old. I was visiting a friend there and as a young model, I had plans that evening to make an appearance at a young, popular nightclub to grace the VIP section with my presence for some promoters. My girls and I spent all evening primping and prepping – polishing nails, doing hair and makeup, picking out our freak 'em dresses, and sharing stories about life in the city and our current love lives. It was late in the evening when we finally decided to head out the door to the venue. I remember looking around and being proud of my three-deep squad, thinking that we were about to set it off. I was the driver for the evening. Our energy was on a high and we were in our own world. We were singing out loud as we blasted the latest crunk music and laughed it up. We were living out our *Sex and the City* fantasy, the Destiny's Child version. After almost thirty minutes of looking for a parking space, I decided I was going to risk it and park in a no-parking zone right next to the door, all for the sake of a good time. We frolicked up to the doors feeling like VIPs, as I gave my name to the host and introduced my friends as my plus three only to have our night shattered by the doorman. He let me know that only *I* was allowed into the club, not because I wasn't allowed any guests but because I was a slim, five-foot-eleven (with heels), model type, and my friends didn't fit the bill. He told us that my friends were not allowed in because of the way they looked. I looked over and noticed that one of my friends was not a tall model type and my other friend, who was tall and stunning by the way, was sporting her natural hair. It was like a scene from a comedy film, where the star of the film tries to fight for their dignity by arguing that it's just a stupid list and that the club wasn't all that good anyway. I was embarrassed and disgusted. I couldn't believe that this was happening. I ended up going inside to see if the promoter could figure out a way to let my friends in but by that time, that had put a damper on the evening and my friends were ready to go. We ended up leaving and trying to save the night by searching for a less pretentious venue. We settled on the fact that that was how New York was, but, no, that was how the world was. We got a reality check on how the world saw us first-hand.

The song "*I Am Not My Hair*," by India Arie is so meaningful, and India captures her natural hair journey well. In the beginning, she sings about the stages of hair: "A little girl with the press and curl / Age eight, I got a Jheri curl / Thirteen, and I got a relaxer ... / At 15 when it all broke off. Eighteen and I went all natural." How many of you can relate? She then goes on to emphasize that she is not her hair but the soul that lives within to highlight that what is on the inside is what will shine through. You are indeed the soul that lives inside of you, which is why you have to first get your mind right before you can focus on the outward person. What is going on in your mind is what will show on the outside. The doorman at that nightclub who rejected my friends was only looking at the physical and didn't acknowledge the fact that they were people with feelings. Rejecting someone because of their physical appearance is hurtful and disrespectful. We are more than what meets the eye, and everyone should be treated with courtesy and respect. Now, India addressed the soul, but three parts make up a person: mind, body, and soul. Seeing that we have a body that goes along with the soul, our appearance and our hair is a reflection of what's going on inside. Our hair is a big part of our culture, our history, and also who we are. We should take care of our bodies just like we take care of our souls. Therefore, we need to make sure that our hair is well maintained and cared for. We are as much black women as we are the souls that live within. Certain characteristics make up human beings, like arms, legs, hands, and feet. Then some things make us different, like our skin color, facial features, and hair. The hair of a white woman will be different from a black woman. Being aware of your differences is okay. Who you are inside does not relinquish any responsibility for the hairstyles you choose. This is like saying that you don't see color, you only see humans, as if noticing that someone differs in skin color is a bad thing. This is simply a way to ignore our differences and apologize for our hair texture. I get where India is going with the song because it starts from within – how you feel about yourself. It says that there is more than what meets the eye, that your feelings, soul, and emotions are what truly make up your character, and true beauty is inside you. It is also true that our soul exists in a physical body and the body is very much you as well. Your hair is a direct reflection of how you feel inside. You are your hair, you are your skin, you are your hips, lips, breast, thighs, and whatever other defining characteristics that make up a woman. You can't deny that you have kinky hair on your head, just as much as you can't deny that you have brown skin or have African ancestry, and why would you? Your hair is your crown, and it should be your pride and joy. Your hair defines who you are, and it makes you the individual that you are, it's as simple as that. This is not to say that there is not more to a person than that, but on a physical level, these help people distinguish you from another human being. You are unique. No one on this earth looks exactly like you. Not even identical twins look exactly the same. When I wore hair weaves, I didn't care for my hair. I thought I was all of that, and I was so cute with a nice wig or a hair weave. I thought my real hair was wild and hard to maintain, but the truth was that I just didn't like my hair and I didn't know how to care for it. I often wore my natural hair intermittently only to get negative reactions from friends and co-workers. My feelings were hurt, and I wasn't strong enough to endure the ugly comments, unapproving looks, and condescending stares. I ended up wearing my wig and weave because that was acceptable and what I thought was more presentable. I didn't want to wear my natural hair because of what other people thought about it, and I was repeating negative thoughts – that my hair was wild and crazy and nappy only because that was what I had heard other people say about my hair. It's time that we stop lying to ourselves. Stop saying, "I don't have good hair," "black hair is not beautiful," "I am not my hair," or "It's just hair." Wake up and realize that you are indeed your hair because your hair is very much a part of you. Your hair is tied to your emotions and how you feel about yourself. Looking at natural hair as a style option is dismissive of what you feel when you decide to wear straight hair, wigs, and weaves. Start saying that your hair is just as good as anyone else's, that it is big and beautiful, and that it's not just hair, it's your crown.

10

IT'S A- SHAME

One day, my husband Dominique decided to share a picture of me on Facebook with a blowout. This lady decided to comment on the post saying that I should take that photo down if I was trying to promote my products because if that was what I was using, it was not working because my hair looked dry. Dominique went on to defend me saying that I was a real, natural black woman and I was beautiful. The lady then posted a photo of a popular natural hair blogger who had a long defined twist-out as if to show me what my hair should have looked like. It was a style that could easily be achieved by a woman with relaxed hair. She just showed me how ignorant she was of natural hair in her preference for one texture over the other. This illustrated the fact that there was now a new struggle among the natural hair community and that was texturism. Texturism is the new word going around that is used to describe when people favor looser, bigger curls over smaller, tighter curls, or the defined natural styles versus the afro-textured styles, respectively. There is a division in the natural hair community where women are focused on defined hair texture and embrace curly and wavy hair but not tightly curled hair. She was shaming me for my fully blown-out afro style because it wasn't a defined twist-out devoid of frizz. When she saw me, she didn't think that I must think highly of myself to wear my hair like that. That I must love my hair. That my hair looked big, luscious, and beautiful. That I was strong, brave, and confident. No, she automatically thought that it was unattractive and the only thing she could say was that it looked dry. Instead of encouraging me for having the courage and the confidence to be myself and not being afraid to show my natural hair, she tried to shame me. When she attempted to put me down, she put down every other black woman who desired to go natural. She put down the black woman's image and affected the self-esteem of every woman reading her comments, because they might have thought that they didn't want to be teased or called a name for being natural, just like when they were a child. The battle between my husband and the lady continued and just went downhill from there. The one thing that my husband did call her out on was the fact that she wore a hair weave. He kept saying that no one knew what her hair looked like because she had a weave. It was really easy for her to criticize my natural hair because she was hiding behind her fake hair. Her comment was not at all helpful or positive, which was what she claimed she was trying to do. Because she never wore her natural hair, she didn't know the difference between a blow-out and a twist-out and that when you have natural hair, sometimes you can wear an afro style or a defined style. In more than one way, what she was saying to me was that she did not think that my big afro hair was beautiful. I'm sure that when she takes down that weave, she has afro hair underneath. So what she was also saying was that she didn't think that she was beautiful either. She didn't think highly of herself and she didn't think highly of black women. She was that bully on the preverbal school playground. Just like the big beauty industry, she was trying to tell me what my hair should look like, she was saying that my hair was nappy. She was wearing the same old tired hair weave that women everywhere wear to cover up who they are and was afraid to show her natural hair but she was quick to criticize mine. She was afraid to be herself. She was afraid to be different from the women in the industry whom everyone wants to emulate. Natural hair is beautiful, no matter how you decide to style it. You need to rock it and be confident, no matter what people say, because most of the haters are insecure trolls who have been persuaded by the big beauty industry to love what is fake and hate what is real. She was brave enough to disapprove of me while she was hiding behind something fake. I later posted a video on YouTube about my disdain for hair weaves and advocacy for black women wearing their natural hair. Black women were so upset with me and defended wearing their hair weaves and wigs as if their lives depended on it. I realized that black women have become so attached to something that is not real. They were uncomfortable being themselves but felt perfectly safe hiding under fake hair. It was the same thing with Beyonce's daughter, Blue Ivy. All of the social media shamed Beyonce for letting her daughter wear her hair naturally. She was a little girl with a cute little afro and everyone on social media felt like it was their place to point out that Beyonce was doing a poor job at grooming her little girl. They made comments that were inappropriate to make about a baby. In essence, they were saying that the child's hair was wild and unkempt. They were shaming Beyonce for letting her daughter wear her natural hair and be herself, instead of encouraging her and every other mother to embrace their daughters 'kinks and curls.

If you find that this is you, demeaning other women, it's time to change your outlook, the way you view yourself, and how you respond to black women who are loving themselves. We are constantly being degraded and our self-worth is constantly being attacked and diminished by the government, men, media, and other people. Start changing the way you think about yourself and the way you see other black women, and you will change the way you treat others. This woman saw me, another black woman who was liberated from trying to have straight, frizz-free hair, and refused to smile at me or encourage me. Instead, she looked down upon me, looked at me crazy, and turned her nose up as if I was making all black women everywhere look bad. She was spreading negative energy about herself everywhere. In reality, she was not happy with herself and was projecting that onto me. You might be the one trolling on social media, being the source of negativity, like the woman on Facebook who tried to texture-shame me. Be kinder toward other people because you're only putting down another queen who looks just like you. Spend more time supporting people and less time demeaning them. You will find that it helps you along your natural hair journey and makes you feel good about yourself in the process. Tell a queen rocking her natural hair that her hair is beautiful and so is she. The energy that will reciprocate will brighten your day.

If you're on the receiving end like I was, don't let someone tell you that you're not good enough; It harms your self-image and makes you feel like you're inferior. Know that there is strength in your strands and that you are strong for not being afraid to own it.

11

NATURAL HAIR IS PROFESSIONAL

During my years in the force, not knowing how to style my natural hair, I began wearing wigs. I wore full wigs and pressed my hair for the rest of my career in the force. After that, when my hair grew long, I decided to experiment with my first hair weave. By this time, I had a good 10 inches of hair, and the first question my hair stylist asked me was, "Why do you want a weave when you have hair?" "I don't know," I told her. "I just want one." Women everywhere praised hair weaves for their versatility and ease of styling and the carefree feeling that came with it. By this time, I was tired of taking care of my hair and I figured after all the years of wearing wigs, I could try a new style where I didn't have to put on and take off the hair every day. I thought having a weave would be easy to maintain and would look good too, but the real answer as to why I wanted a hair weave was because I was still trying to be that white woman I saw on the television. After that first installation of a hair weave, I was hooked. I no longer cared for my hair and its texture or growth. I was able to buy any type of hair I wanted and change my look anytime I felt like it and it was fun. I spent years and thousands of dollars getting my good hair weaves and didn't think twice about the hair underneath. It became a normal thing for me to get hair weaves and I looked good with them, so I was happy. Occasionally, I would give my hair a so-called break by getting a press and curl, but soon after I was right back to wearing a weave. I was later introduced to partial hair weaves, where I could leave some of my real hair out in the front and make it as straight as possible to match the weaved texture for a more "natural" looking weave. I later tried a lace front wig because that was the trendiest and the most natural-looking hair wig at the time. Meanwhile, my hair was being neglected, breaking off, and growing limp and frail, but it didn't bother me. I was constantly covering it up with a hair weave. I remember one day I had taken out my hair weave and also the braids that were underneath, but I didn't comb out my hair. So when one of the beauticians at the salon washed my hair, it became matted and knotted up to the point where it looked like matted dreadlocks all over my head. The beautician didn't know that she should have detangled my hair before she washed it, but now we were stuck with a big mess. So she began ripping through my hair with a fine-tooth comb, literally pulling hair from my scalp. She was working so hard that she needed to take a break in between the wrestle with my afro. It took her all of thirty minutes to comb out all of the knots in my hair. By the end, my head was throbbing with pain. In the end, I was left with thin and uneven strands of damaged hair. Not knowing any better myself, I was so grateful for her putting in all that work that I gave her a twenty-dollar tip. I couldn't care less about the health of my hair. I was more concerned about getting a fresh weave. For years, that was all I did – hair weaves with the occasional press and curl, and I continued to remain uninformed on how my hair choices affected the way I felt about myself. It took some time for me to heal, but the first thing I needed to do was fix it. Ideally, it should be the other way around, where wearing natural hair is the norm because all black women have it and should be wearing it all the time, but unfortunately, that's not how it is.

After I left the Air Force, I got a job as a secretary working with the Department of Justice. I worked in a building with a majority of middle-aged white males and a handful of black people. My department seemed to be where the government met its quota for affirmative action since that was where they grouped all of the token black folks and one person of Latin descent, all in one department. Of course, the department leader was a country-talking middle-aged white man from West Virginia to help keep us in line. He insisted that we call him by his last name, even though everyone was on a first name basis, and also because he used initials for his first name, which were the initials A. G. We always asked him what the initials stood for and he would tell us they spelled out to "All Good." Let's call him Joe.

I had been wearing my regular wigs and weaves to work with no problems. I would always receive compliments on every style, be it a flat-ironed style or a weave, or an occasional wig. I remember one time one of the older white men in the office, with his old-fashioned form of flattery, commented that I looked very stylish, like Diana Ross. Now don't get me wrong, I love Diana Ross but what he was saying was my wig looked dated, and I will admit, I had a cheap synthetic wig that I bought from the local beauty supply. No offense to Diana, but this was 2008 and wigs had come a long way since Diana's day. One day, after I washed my hair and was feeling adventurous, I decided to wear it naturally. I walked into my office and immediately felt the tension. I started getting funny looks from the men in the office and there was a thick silence. My hair became the elephant in the room. Throughout the day, I noticed that people were treating me differently and would ask me questions like "Are you okay?" and I started to feel like I had made a big mistake. Later that day, Joe called me into his office along with another co-worker for what I thought was to discuss our upcoming project. But to my surprise, the first question he asked me was, "What the hell happened to your hair?" I stood there dumbfounded and embarrassed as the other man next to me burst into laughter. I didn't know whether to go off on him, storm out of his office, or simply explain to him what had happened. I decided upon the latter. I simply explained that I had washed my hair and had decided not to straighten it. Then he followed up with an even more invasive question, "Well, how does your boyfriend like it?" Now that was when I should have gone off and told him that it was none of his business, but I remained calm and retorted, "Yes, my boyfriend loves it." I don't know how the conversation went after that but he proceeded to talk shop. The rest of the conversation was awkward and unsettling. I felt like crap for the rest of the day. After the summons to Joe's office, word got around quickly. I kept getting strange reactions to my hair. People were coming down to my desk to peek over at me, making silly comments like, "Do we have a new person?" and "Who's the new girl?" The handful of token black people whom I thought would have my back were shocked and surprised also. I felt alone, ashamed, and excluded. I realized that many people – both black and white – had never seen a black woman with her natural hair. So, of course, I got stared at and received some disapproving looks from black people. Of course, people are going to look at you differently and that might be your biggest fear – wondering what people will say, what they will think, and how they will treat you. Well, I did get some negative and some positive reactions, but the ironic thing was that people had negative and positive reactions to the way I looked even before I decided to wear my natural hair. The only difference was that I was more confident hiding behind a hair weave or straight hair. I realized that people were going to form opinions regardless of the way I wore my hair. The thing that I needed to possess was the self-confidence to demand respect from others. I realized that confidence was key. I wish I could have shared the story about how I stuck it to the white man or how I saw this as the chance to educate the world on who a real black woman was, but I felt so defeated that I decided to go back to wearing my hair straight the following day. Even after the natural hair movement within the black community which led to women no longer using chemical straighteners, straightening tools, and hair weaves, we still suffer anxiety around hair issues and spend more on hair care than our white peers. A new study confirms that many people — including black ones — have a bias against the types and styles of natural hair worn by black people. They are almost twice as likely to experience social pressure at work to straighten their hair compared to white women. They are even asked to cut their dreadlocks or trim their big afros. Wearing your natural hair takes confidence and courage. Given our history in the United States, where our hair has been deemed unprofessional and unkept, wearing our natural hair is making a statement and challenging the shame that exists around black hair. When you wear your natural hair, you are telling the media, government, and everyone else that you are not afraid to be an individual and you are not going to conform to the media and the big beauty industry's idea of what beauty is. So, get ready to represent and let them know that natural hair is acceptable, even in the workplace.

12

YOU'RE WALKING AROUND WITHOUT YOUR CROWN

Crowning glory *(phrase)* - the most interesting or important thing that something or someone has to offer.

Our hair is often referred to as our crowning glory, considering that our hair sits on the top of our head and we dress it and adorn it with the best hairstyles and accessories. We spend countless hours and hundreds of dollars to make sure that our hair is on point. It has always been a source of pride and joy, but we've manipulated our hair to the point where our crown is unrecognizable. I was reading an article online from a guy who was talking about Solange's album *A Seat at the Table,* namely the track *Don't Touch my Hair.* He was saying that she, "opened his eyes" when it came to realizing why black women were going natural and what going natural meant to black women. He said that when she used the word "crown" to describe her natural tresses, it put everything into perspective on how going natural involved a sense of pride in one's culture and was not just a choice of hairstyle. Black women have been saying, "My hair is my crown," but haven't been wearing it. Are you rocking your crown? Or are you wearing your insecurities as your crown? If you refer to your hair as your crowning glory – which is the most interesting or important thing that you have to offer – then own what makes you uniquely you. We've been walking around without our crowns and now white America has come to police our hair. It's no coincidence that black women are being excluded on purpose. We need to step up and show the world our beauty, so much so that we can't be ignored. Considering that our hair is a sign of liberation that may be offensive to a racist society, there is going to be some opposition, which is what has been happening. There are rules and regulations in the workplace and in school systems that prevent us from wearing our afro hair texture and ethnic hairstyles like braids, twists, and cornrows. Young girls have been kicked off of sports teams and restricted from going to their senior prom because of their hairstyles. The Supreme Court passed a law that restricted dreadlocks in the workplace with the threat of getting fired if you decided to don your locks. There have been many instances of black girls, and women being racially profiled and even attacked at school or work because of their hair. A seven-year-old girl's head was shaved by a volunteer at a group home called Little Heroes in Dracut, Massachusetts, and one of the volunteers told the little girl that her hair would grow back straight. Pause. Yes, ma'am. This is a true story. Can you imagine how traumatized both the mother and the daughter were after this incident? Natural hair should not be tampered with. People should not be bullied because of the way they decide to wear their hair. Another incident took place at Mystic Valley Regional Charter School in Malden, Massachusetts when two students were kicked out of class because they were told that their extensions were distractions. Other students at this school who wore their hair in its natural state were told that they would have to perm or chemically straighten it. The parents of these children showed the administration pictures of Caucasian girls with extensions, but they were told their extensions weren't noticeable. The black students were given two options – either to comply with the school rule to straighten their hair, drop out, or get kicked out. That is so unfair. When schools attempt to implement things like this, it strips the confidence of young black children and infringes upon our rights. A young black man's dreads had to be cut off for him to graduate, a young lady was expelled from school for wearing her braids, and the list goes on. Why do we have to change our hair, while everyone else can walk around with their natural hair? Why is straight hair depicted as more professional and curly hair deemed as unruly or untamed? People should not be judged by their hair type, shape, color, length, etc. But, unfortunately, we are. When children are told to change their hair to look more Caucasian, it strips away their identity. Telling black students to change their natural hair also tells them that there's a problem with their hair. The hair that grows out of these children's heads is a problem, but when it's growing out of Caucasian children's heads, it isn't an issue. There's something very wrong with that. As black people, we are already barely accepted in places because of the color of our skin, but to be put out of school for the way we wear our hair is unjust and discriminatory, to say the least. Learning to embrace the coily, or curly aspects of your hair is important for reasons like being discriminated against. Teaching your children how important it is to love their hair will make them stand up to the craziness. Changing your hair should be a choice that you make on your own, not a choice that the administration at a school or your boss imposes on you. Natural hair is beautiful in every state, and if more people from different backgrounds understood that, it wouldn't be deemed as unruly or as a distraction. Natural hair is a part of our culture, and when people of other ethnicities are in our presence, we don't demand that they fix or change their hair. We deserve that same respect in return. Thankfully, there's The CROWN Act. CROWN stands for Creating a Respectful and Open World for Natural hair. It was created by Dove and The CROWN Coalition in 2019 to prevent discrimination against black natural hair and ethnic hairstyles in the workplace and schools. This is the first of its kind and so far, seven states have signed the bill into law, which includes California, Washington, Colorado, New York, New Jersey, Maryland, and Virginia. They are steadily making progress to prevent discrimination against black hair, but there need to be protections not only in all fifty states in the United States but also all over the world. It's a shame that we even need a bill to prevent the regulation of our hair, but one of the things that you can do is participate in this change by visiting thecrownact.com and signing to bring the bill into law in your state. The best thing that you can do is simply wear your natural hair as a bold statement against the system that wants to regulate it. Unlike other cultures, we have a uniquely rich history when it comes to our hairstyles, along with a rich history of oppression. Black women have always been told how to style their hair to appease the white race. You can start choosing your hair and showing the white society that black hair is not something that they can control.

PART THREE

YOUR STRENGTH

13

NATURAL HAIR REVOLUTION

"As a black woman, the decision to love yourself just as you are is a radical act." - Bethanee Epifani J. Bryant

Black women were not allowed to show their natural hair, were getting paid less than their white female and male counterparts, and were being told that they were too dark and too curvy. We were later forced to change the texture of our hair, character, and entire identity to assimilate into the American culture. As a result, we, as black women, have learned to resent our hair and see it as unattractive and unpleasant, but because of the damage that chemical relaxers have on our hair and scalp, in addition to the change in our perspective of ourselves, we are learning to love our hair and are finding ways to care for it. The natural hair movement started when black women decided to stop getting hair relaxers and wearing wigs and weaves and decided to wear our natural hair. Relaxer sales have dropped in the past five years and there has been an increase in natural hair products on the market. Over the past several years, black women have been thriving due to the natural hair movement. We are freeing ourselves physically and mentally from Eurocentric ideas of what we should strive to emulate. We are shining in our glory and it's because we've finally decided to love who we are. The awakening has happened, but some women are still asleep and some are drifting back to sleep. You may not know where to start, but with the Internet, natural hair salons, and all the new products popping up on the market everywhere, there is no excuse. Rid yourself of the mundane and restrictive life of hair weaves, wigs, and relaxers, and discover the feeling and independent life of a natural woman. I will be honest, I didn't dare to return natural on my own. I attempted to wear my hair out in between hair weaves but I would regularly straighten it or wear a wig because I wasn't quite comfortable wearing my natural hair. I was looking for permission to wear it and it wasn't until I had gotten the encouragement of my husband that I finally realized why I should be rocking my afro. After being married for several months, my husband, Dominique, saw my natural hair for the first time after I took down my hair weave and washed my hair. He fell in love with the texture and the curl pattern and saw the beauty in it way before I did. He suggested that I wear it out natural. I kept opposing him due to all of the negative comments and thoughts that I had heard and continue to hear about natural hair. Due to all the negative associations with my natural hair, I ultimately felt that it was something bad to be ashamed of and hide. Then, after I began to hear all of the positive words that he was saying about my hair, I started to take another look and realized that it wasn't as bad as I had thought. I also realized that I was talking badly not only about my hair but also about myself. I was putting myself down. It took hours of arguing for him to finally convince me that my hair was beautiful and that I could wear it out if I took the time to style it and manage it properly. When I decided to go natural and *stay* natural, it was after Dominque spent hours trying to convince me that my hair was beautiful and that I should wear it natural all the time. He was the first person to tell me so, partly because I had never really worn my natural hair out with conviction and partly because the people around me never really felt that way. I had to think about why I was wearing weaves and straight hair. The reason was that I thought that my natural black hair was not good enough. We have been told that it was unsightly, that we were animals, that we were less than other races. We were demeaned for decades and we have heard those negative comments for so long that we believe them and that was why we have to work to change it. It wasn't until that point in my life that I saw my hair for what it was, tightly curled. I began to explore it more. I changed the way I thought about my hair: I thought there was nothing wrong with my hair. This was the hair I was born with. Why couldn't I just be myself? I wanted to be who I was born to be, the way God made me. It was then that I finally change my mindset. It wasn't just about hair for me, it was about taking back my self-esteem and saying "no" to anything false. I started saying "yes" to myself and embracing who I was. I stopped apologizing for the way my hair looked, and I stopped making excuses as to why I couldn't be natural. I decided to choose myself. After I decided to return to natural and *stay* natural, I was more confident in who I was. I was a different person. I felt free. It was freeing because I could finally live my life being myself. It's a feeling that all black women should know and share. That moment was so inspiring that I decided to make a short film about it entitled *Naturally Free,* about a woman who rediscovers her natural hair. I wrote the film because I wanted to express to other black women that it's time to be free. There was a feeling of being liberated when I decided to wear my natural hair and stopped hiding under a wig or weave, which can be considered a part of the masks that you put on every day. I started to take ownership of the woman that I was. It was liberating because I finally accepted myself for who I was. It was liberating because I decided not to let outsiders influence how I felt about myself and what I considered to be beautiful. After being married for a year, we then decided to have children. I was pregnant with our first child, Alexander, and decided to transition to a "clean" lifestyle. I was cautious about the things that I put in and on my body. That was when I discovered the harmful chemicals in baby products. They were the same as the toxic ingredients in a lot of beauty products, so that was when I started making natural products for my skin and hair that my baby and I could use. I now have two children, my youngest being a little girl named Kiah, and she wears her beautiful curls proudly. Wearing my natural hair has inspired me in so many ways. It inspired me to write a film, it inspired the creation of my natural hair and skincare brand, JOSHICA

BEAUTY, and it inspires me to keep pushing for change every time I see my beautiful children. I created a brand of natural hair care products because I wanted to find natural ways to take care of my hair. Products without harmful chemicals and that were good to use in my afro-textured hair. I also created products so that women with hair like mine can have options for what to use in their hair. I wanted to motivate women to go natural and to give their natural hair a chance. It is about growing your self-worth and realizing how much of a statement your hair makes in this world. It's about growing healthy hair and growing a healthy relationship with yourself. You can't be happy if you don't even like who you are. Learn to accept things the way they are and stop thinking that what you have is not good. What you have is great and it's time for you to realize it. You have to do the work and take the time to invest in yourself. No one can do it for you. Stop telling yourself that you are not acceptable and that you are not attractive with your natural hair, by putting on a wig or weaving or wearing your hair straight. Start telling yourself that you are lovely and amazing by wearing your natural hair. It took a big argument between Dominique and me for me to realize that my behavior and my thoughts toward myself were destructive. I couldn't recognize the problem with wearing a weave and the deeper impact that it had on my self-esteem. Dominique wasn't even trying to be the one to teach me a valuable life lesson. He just told me the truth and showered me with positivity. It wasn't until I started to listen and pay attention to what he was saying that I made the change. I was hurting myself with those words and thoughts. I was being my bully, like the media and social media trolls, that tells me that I am not attractive and that needed to stop. I told myself that I wasn't going to think like that anymore or continue to put myself down. That I was going to refuse a weave, wig, and relaxed hair, even if it killed me because I didn't want to hurt my self-esteem and feel dependent on some external object to mask a hurt that stemmed from my childhood. I didn't want to return to that sunken place of thinking that I had to be like the women on television who were an inaccurate and modified representation of black women or white. I didn't want fake hair to define me, to be my crutch or cover-up. I wanted the world to see the new me. I wanted to come out into my own and live a life without fear of being discovered. I wanted to live a life just being the little girl I was before the world started to chip away at my self-worth. Natural black hair is more than hair. It's about an evolution toward self-love and self-empowerment. It's about a mindset that you are not going to conform to society's view of beauty, and you are going to set your standard. It shows that you are not afraid to stand out and be who you are. It shows that you are comfortable with your self-image and that you are confident in who you are. Your natural hair is a revolution because of how you have been viewed in this country. When you wear your natural hair, you show up and resist the world's view of beauty. Some women don't want to admit that it is a natural hair movement because they don't think that changing their hairstyle is that serious, but the truth is that black women going natural is a worldwide movement, that is not only showing the world that black women are beautiful but also rebelling against the industry's view of beauty. You might feel that there are more important things in the world that we should be concerned about, like Black Lives Matter, police brutality, and mass incarceration. Those are things that you can support and participate in but those are things that you may or may not have the ability to change. Focus your energy on the things that are within your control and see what you can do to change them. If your hair is a sign of protest, then wear your natural hair and show that black lives do, in fact, matter, and our culture, style, and hairdo too. When you wear your natural hair out, you are saying to the big beauty industry, "No, I will not follow the crowd. No, I will not take your beauty advice. No, I will not let you tell me what beauty is, and no, I will not buy what you're selling." You are ultimately saying, "This is what beauty is. This is who I am, and you better recognize it because I'm not apologizing for it." Now the tables are turning. Black women are now telling the beauty industry and the entertainment industry what we want, while they are trying their hardest to cater to us. We are a part of a movement, a movement that is changing the beauty industry and the way the world looks at black women forever. So be a part of it. Be a part of the movement of rediscovering your beauty, acknowledging it, and making the world acknowledge it too.

14

RETURNING NATURAL

"Do the best you can do until you know better. Then when you know better, you do better." - Maya Angelou

We are ever evolving and growing, which is why we often refer to life as a journey. It is your job to learn and grow from life lessons along the way. Now that you can see how the beauty industry is profiting off your low self-esteem and how your hair choices ignore a deeper hurt, it's time to pivot. You don't have to stay where you are. Learn to grow and be unafraid to give yourself a chance. More women, now more than ever, are starting to wake up and realize the truth that our hair is one of the most beautiful things we can possess as black women. It's not the hips, butt, thighs, or full lips that make you a rare beauty, it's the bountiful and bold crown of hair that stands out in any crowd and says, "I'm black and beautiful and I am not ashamed."

You might not think highly of your natural hair because you have heard negative thoughts about your physical appearance. You have to first work on getting rid of those thoughts before you can move forward to try to accept and love your natural hair. Your love for yourself and your positive energy reflects from the inside out. Look at yourself in the mirror and start to think and say positive things about your hair. Let's face it, you can't love yourself if you don't even accept your hair texture. If you don't love yourself, you are redirecting those negative thoughts and energy to yourself and the rest of the world. You wouldn't want to be around someone who talks badly about your hair all the time, but that is exactly what you are doing to yourself and the women around you. Your hair texture is one of the things that make you unique as a black woman and you should look at that as a blessing, not a curse. You have hair that is unique, bold and stands out to the point where white women are changing the texture of their hair to pass as black. Everyone knows that black women have afro-textured hair. You don't know what it means to be confident and walk in your truth if you're constantly lying to yourself by telling yourself that your hair is ugly, and you need a weave or straight hair to look and feel attractive. Stop telling yourself those things. Stop speaking that negativity into your life. You haven't begun to reach your full potential until you find the courage to face yourself. You have to be brave enough to be different and do something that scares you. Do something different from what other people have told you and what you are accustomed to. Don't believe the lies about your hair, such as that it is ugly, big, wild, messy, needs straightening, makes you look like a slave, or that it's too much to take care of. The more women that return natural, the more I hear stories about how they were told that their hair was ugly, unkempt, or unpresentable and needed to be fixed or tamed. Black women with natural hair should be the norm. We shouldn't need books or films to tell us that our natural hair is beautiful and that we are beautiful. We shouldn't require the world's approval or constant encouragement to remind us of our natural beauty, but as long as there is a beauty industry that offers opposing views, we need to constantly let each other know that we are beautiful. We may never have a film that depicts a beautiful black woman as the lead actress whom everyone fights to save because she is precious, beautiful, and valued. We may never get songs written about our beautiful, bountiful curls and coils that adorn our heads like a crown given to us from heaven above. We may never be given a few pages in a history book about how our natural tresses changed the world. But they will know that black women loved themselves and lived unapologetically. As we shift toward building ourselves, we are creating a community of proud black women who can't be ignored.

Straight hair has always been the trend because that is what is popular in the media. White women have always been popular when it comes to the beauty industry, but we are creating our own beauty culture and that includes us in our natural state. Now that black women are starting to wake up to the fact that wearing European styles is disrespectful to our own culture, we are reclaiming our space and showing up as the proud black women that we are. Now black women are setting the trends and we are the face of beauty. Our hair reflects our history and sets the tone for the future. Our natural hair shouldn't be subdued. Now black women are starting to realize that our hair is beautiful. We are changing the way we think about ourselves. Remember, then when you know better, you do better.

15

FREE YOUR MIND AND YOUR HAIR WILL FOLLOW

"Whatever we believe about ourselves and our ability comes true for us." - Susan L. Taylor

The mind is a powerful thing. It allows you to change the course of your life and set you on a path of self-awareness. You can start becoming aware of where you are and who you are when you approach things from a positive perspective instead of a negative point of view. How you see yourself is how you are going to be. Returning natural requires more than just doing the big chop and changing your hairstyle. It requires you to change what's inside your head before you can change what's on top of your head. Taking care of your natural hair is simple. It's just a matter of finding the right product and style, but you have to first have the desire to work with your hair and learn to understand it. It starts with a choice to invest in yourself and invest in self-care. Learn to change the way you think about your hair by speaking positive things to yourself and preventing negative thoughts about your hair from coming in. Learn to block out all of the things that you heard growing up or continue to hear, and start to speak the truth into your present. The truth is that your hair is tightly curled and prone to dryness. It defies gravity and is versatile. Once you've accepted the truth, you will know how to deal with things moving forward. Don't ignore what is in front of you. When you change your hair texture to appease someone else, you ignore a deeper truth. You choose to hide behind a more acceptable image of yourself. Allowing yourself to see yourself as beautiful requires you to realign your thoughts on the positive instead of the negative. Start seeing yourself as attractive and your hair as your crown. Something that you are willing to learn more about. Stop looking at your hair as a burden that you have to take care of and start looking at it as an opportunity to get to know yourself better. Don't be afraid to try something new and different and don't give up on yourself. You might look at natural hair as a job and be overwhelmed with the time and attention it takes to make it look a certain way. Instead of thinking that your natural hair is something that you *have* to take care of, look at it as something that you *get* to take care of, and first be grateful for what you do have. If something doesn't work well for you in the beginning, you can always revisit it later, but don't give up. This is only *yourself*, you're investing in. It might be hard to figure out your hair but that is what natural hair stylists are for. You can get help in finding a style and learning how to maintain your hair, just like you do with straight hair. After you start to speak positive things to yourself, you will start to believe them. Your mindset has to change for you to change your hairstyle and your overall lifestyle. The change does not start with your hair, it starts in your mind. We need to get back to loving ourselves. Get back to shouting, "I'm black, and I'm proud!" We need to let go of our fear and worry about what other people might think, and how we may hurt someone's feelings or offend others with how we look. If other people have a problem with you being yourself, then you shouldn't concern yourself with other people's problems. You have to understand that you have to free yourself from mental captivity. You are trapped in a box that someone else has set for you. Some might say that if all black women went natural, then we'll be putting ourselves in a constraint, as if we can't be free to wear weaves, wigs, or straight hair, but it's the opposite. You are freeing yourself. You are allowing yourself to be genuine and not confined to a shell of yourself. When you are unafraid to be yourself, you are making a bold statement. You are rebelling against the norm and the limits that have been placed on you. You are stepping out of the box and stepping into your space.

Most black women have a type-4 hair texture and that is the tightest and driest hair texture on the hair texture chart. Your hair is not going to look like a type-3 hair texture or a looser s-curl, so you are going to have to learn to love *your* texture. Unless you add toxic chemicals, no product or hairstyle will magically change your hair texture and give you a head full of big bouncy loose curls. To learn to love yourself, you need to make an honest assessment of yourself to determine where you are today. Clarify your values and what is important to you.

You are always changing, and the good thing is that you can become a different person with the change of your mindset. If you have self-awareness and can identify where you are now, then you can figure out if you need to change your thinking to live a better life. You can start a self-assessment by asking yourself why:

Why do I feel the way I do about my hair?
Why do I wear my hair the way I do?

After you've asked yourself these questions, be truthful with yourself to make an honest assessment of where you are. When you can determine where you are, then you start to build confidence in yourself. Discovering who you are is achievable if you continually work toward it.

16

THE BOLD AND THE BEAUTIFUL

"There is nothing more beautiful than a woman being unapologetically herself, comfortable in her perfect imperfection." - Steve Maraboi

Women everywhere are beginning to realize that we have been lied to, hoodwinked, and bamboozled! Whoever told us that our hair was not beautiful was straight-up lying, which is no surprise. Stop putting up with the long hours in the salons, the chemicals that damage your hair and scalp, and the expensive wigs that ultimately conceal your natural beauty. Begin to realize that your hair is perfect for you. No one on this earth has hair like ours and we should embrace our differences and not be ashamed.

One day, a guy told me that he loved my natural hair because he could see my ears. I thought that was odd but it's interesting the things that people notice about you that you would never notice about yourself. He went on to explain that when women wear hair weaves and wigs, it covers their ears. So wearing natural hair makes you appreciate the little things, like a woman's ears. Men want a woman who is real. Of course, men want a woman who is happy with whatever she does but a woman who is confident in her skin is something that men want because if you don't love yourself, it shows. My husband told me that I turned into a different person after I started wearing my natural hair. He proclaimed that I had changed into this new person who was more confident and sure of herself. I started living like a queen. I've heard women say that when they went natural, they started to attract a different kind of man. Not that you go natural to attract attention from men, but men and women do notice when you are sure of yourself. When a woman is sure of herself, she attracts attention, the good kind. She demands respect and lives a more fulfilled life.

Black women everywhere are waking up to the fact that wearing wigs and weaves is an ignominy to our culture and can be detrimental to our health. Recently, several celebrities decided to cut all of their hair off and even go bald to start their natural hair journey. R&B singer Tamar Braxton posted on her social media that she cut her hair because she was tired of being a slave to wigs and weaves; she wanted to be herself. Viola Davis started her natural journey and said she wanted to stop apologizing for who she was. Sana Lathan cut her hair for the film *Nappily Ever After*, an inspiring film about a woman coming into her own and starting her natural hair journey. Comedian Tiffany Haddish shaved her head, just so she could see her scalp. Unfortunately, when celebrities go natural, they end up going right back to their hair wigs and weaves because the industry does not favor their natural hair. You might look at that as a sign that black hair is unfavorable, and that *you* should go back to wearing wigs, weaves, and straight hair as well. Just when you thought they were embracing their blackness, here they go wearing wigs and weaves on set and stage. They did manage to get one thing right by speaking out about freeing themselves from the bondage of wigs and weaves and how it could cause women to lose their hair and damage our value.

The act of going natural has meant many different things: going natural, natural hair journey, returning natural, awakening, the natural hair movement, and that natural hair revolution. All these different titles are starting to sound like Hollywood movies. Regardless of what you call it, black women everywhere are starting to realize that our hair *is* gorgeous, You are alluring and you have made the mistake of covering up and perming your natural hair all these years.

Be the woman God created you to be. You were "fearfully and wonderfully made" and everything that God made is good. Don't insult the beautiful design of the Creator. You were sculpted from head to toe and your hair is a uniquely beautiful creation that adds to the awesomeness of being a black woman. Own your uniqueness. Acknowledge what makes you different and don't hide what is meant to display greatness. Allow yourself permission to flourish. If you give your love to those you care about, you deserve that same love. When you look around and see the different ethnicities all across the world, most of them have the same features; light skin, straight hair, and slim body types, but not black women. We stand out. We have dark skin, thick, big hair, curves, and full features. Everything about us stands out and that is a wonderful thing. You can't be afraid to stand out. You were meant to stand out naturally, so be your natural self. Don't be afraid to be yourself. There is nothing really to be afraid of because people are going to judge you and think whatever they want, regardless of how you carry yourself and how you style your hair. You have to live your life being free from what others think. You have to live your life being the person you were designed to be. Be confident in yourself and know that it is perfectly okay to wear an afro without feeling ashamed. Some cultures might be offended because of their racist views, but that should never stop you from being yourself and living your life freely. Stop pretending to be someone you are not. When you put on a wig or weave, it's like putting on a mask; you try to tone down your hairstyle and you end up toning down yourself to please someone else. You have to start living. Start living for yourself and not for the people on your job, your friends, your family, or people who don't feel comfortable with you being yourself. Yes, our natural hair is big; big hair is sexy, but if you're not a fan of big hair, then you could always start with a natural hairstyle that attracts less attention like a twist-out, braids, or a sculpted up-do – you have so many options. Our hair is extremely flexible and fun to play with. I like to think of our hair as a sculpture. It may take time to mold and shape but in the end, it will turn out to be a work of art. This is something that black women everywhere are waking up to. They are learning to embrace their hair. We are, in turn, building the self-worth of black women everywhere. When you realize that you have been influenced to think less of yourself, it's time for a shift. You no longer need to let someone determine your worth and manipulate your self-esteem. It's time to think highly of yourself. Women who wear their natural hair are brave and have a healthy relationship with their self-image. They are not afraid to be the person they were created to be. Step out of the shadows. Stop hiding and be naturally free.

17

KNOWING YOUR SELF-WORTH

"It isn't where you come from; it's where you're going that counts." - Ella Fitzgerald

The importance of knowing yourself and being at peace with who you are cannot be emphasized enough. This can take some trial and error, and you will constantly learn new things about yourself, but it is a journey that should be undertaken with purpose and zeal. Turn self-hate into self-love

Taking care of your hair is a form of self-care. Taking care of your hair is not the only way to take care of yourself but it shows yourself, love. You're doing something that will benefit your physical and mental well-being. If you can't make yourself feel right, how can you expect to help with someone else's problems? Get your mind right before you try to volunteer your time and energy to help with the world's problems. When it comes to loving your hair, make sure you're regularly deep conditioning your hair, getting steam treatments, gently detangling, and sleeping with a stain cap. Pamper your hair and learn to take care of it as a part of self-care. One way that you can learn to be confident in your skin is by going to a professional natural hairstylist. Even though there may not be many natural hair salons in your area, try to find a beautician who specializes in natural hair that can give you a hair consultation on your hair texture, type, and the treatments and services you might need. You should always look for feedback on how to maintain your hair. You can always ask a friend. Even though it's a growing market, unfortunately, there may not be many beauticians who specialize in natural hair. Considering the number of natural hair bloggers and natural hair enthusiasts experimenting with their natural hair, they may know more about your natural hair texture than most cosmetologists. Ask a friend for advice and tips on how to maintain and talk about how you feel about your hair and how they feel about theirs. Taking care of your hair is taking care of your body, so while you're maintaining your natural hair, don't forget to exercise, drink plenty of water, eat your vegetables, and do healthy things that you enjoy doing.

Learning to accept yourself requires you to learn to accept your looks. The images that are being portrayed in the media have allowed you to hate yourself long enough. Instead of believing the lies that you are inferior and unattractive, know that you have amazing hair that is multifaceted, powerful, and unique. You are beautiful and it is time that you start believing that instead. You have to change your way of thinking and no one can make that change except you.

I've mentioned how the media and people might have influenced you to have negative thoughts, but other factors influence you to make decisions about your hair and may deter you from going natural. These are your age, illnesses, disabilities, physical limitations, and your job. Genetics can shape your personality but it is often your experiences. Your family environment can also be the reason for your hair choices because of your social and economic conditions which lead you to not being able to afford to take care of your natural hair or think it's less classy to have natural hair. You constantly receive this overly critical negative assessment of your hair from friends and family, which makes it hard for you to change. You might feel that you don't need to wear your natural hair when you are already winning and you are happy with the person that you are, but do you know who you are? Have you taken the time to look at yourself in the mirror and say to yourself, "I love you? You're beautiful, you are enough, you are growing, you make a difference in this world?" When I decided to wear my natural hair, I just thought, "forget it, this is me. You can take it or leave it. You either like me or you don't. If you think I'm cool, then we're cool. If you're not feeling my hair, then you can keep it moving." I had to accept my physical appearance to accept who I was.

Take inventory - Write down 10 things you like about your hair and 10 things you don't like. This will help you to begin developing an honest and realistic idea of yourself. This will allow you to become more self-aware and open about how you feel about yourself. One of the things that I love about my hair is the curly pattern, especially when it is wet. I also love the versatility of my natural hair. Some of the things that I don't like are how it gets matted up when I lay down and how it attracts lint. After you have assessed how you feel about your hair and the negative self-talk, you need to let go of those feelings and start thinking positively.

Set realistic expectations. It's important to set small, reachable goals that are within your power. Start small by adding a new product to your regimen or trying out a new natural style for a week, just to get a feel for what your hair can do, before you fully commit, and just accept that everyone is not going to be happy with your decisions.

Not everyone is on your side. After I decided to return natural and *stay* natural, I went to work at my job where Dominique and I had first met. I was met by awkward stares and snickering once again. My supervisor made a comment that I looked like "Sideshow Bob" who was another white guy, but I had prepared myself for the unwanted comments from my new co-workers and the disapproving looks I would receive from my peers. I knew that I had to not feed into anyone indifferent to me choosing to be myself and correct those who crossed the line.

One day, I took my two children to visit my 85-year-old grandmother. My daughter had her beautiful curly afro. When my grandmother saw her, she asked what I was going to do with my daughter's hair. I told her, "Nothing. I like her afro the way it is." She then frowned and told me that it was *nappy* and that I needed to braid it up. My daughter's hair is a soft loose s-curl, the type of texture that most black women would love to have, and her little two-year-old afro was the cutest thing you could have ever seen, but to my grandmother, it was *nappy*, it was unkept, it needed to be changed. It was hard for me to explain to my grandmother that her hair was beautiful like that and that saying things like that was hurtful. She was set in her way of thinking and I realized that she had been taught those things all her life and her views on black hair were not going to change.

Just like the woman who criticized me about my afro, there will always be people who oppose black hair, even our people. But don't let other people make you feel that you have to be perfect all the time when it comes to your natural hair. Don't let anyone try to shame you into thinking that you are making a mistake by choosing yourself. You are taking care of yourself and that is not selfish; it's self-care. Some people are going to be persistent in telling you how crazy they think you look with your natural hair, and you are going to have to ignore the noise and not internalize such negative comments.

Sometimes it will be the ones closest to you who will hurt you the most. They feel comfortable enough to say whatever is on their minds and to judge the way you look. You have to let them know that your natural hair is the real you, that you are choosing yourself, and that you are happy with yourself. They are going to have to accept you for who you are because that is how you chose to live. Unfortunately, you would have to explain to people why you decide to be yourself and not hate your hair, but that is the society we live in. They should be supportive of your decisions to better yourself and discover who you are. They may or may not get it, but they are going to have to learn to embrace it if they want to continue a healthy relationship with you. Setting an expectation that someone else will change their behavior is virtually guaranteed to make you feel like a failure, through no fault of your own. The sad truth is that a lot of people are just not going to get it. Most women are comfortable with the choices they have made to make their hair look European. Most women are not ready to wake up. It may take longer for someone to understand the reason behind their choices. Live the rest of your life knowing that you are not inferior and that you have something to offer to this world. To do so, you may have to start over and that means with relationships too.

Stop being a perfectionist and acknowledge both your accomplishments and mistakes. Nobody is perfect. Trying to be perfect will only lead to disappointment. Acknowledging your accomplishments and recognizing your mistakes is the way to keep a positive outlook while learning and growing from your mistakes. Everyone is not on the same journey and some people may choose to remain asleep. Now that you know that you have not been accepting of yourself, it's time to make a change. You may have lived your entire life not appreciating yourself, but you know now, that you don't want to continue to remain a slave to the white ideology that says that white people have superiority. Replace working toward perfectionism with working to get better each day. Say to yourself, "Each day, and in every way, I'm getting better and better and better." Congratulate yourself for choosing to let go of the offensive things in your past, so that you can heal and live a happier and more fulfilled life, knowing who you are. Don't focus on the things that are not going to make you feel good about yourself. Instead, focus on what you are good at and celebrate the small successes and the progress you are making with your hair and your self-respect.

Explore your hair. Try a wash-and-go style to see what type of curl pattern your hair has or learn to do a two-strand twist to see how well your hair holds. Figure out what you are good at when it comes to style. Can you braid? Can you twist? Are you patient with detangling? Our hair is like a work of art, it may take time to sculpt and shape it, but it comes out looking like a masterpiece. Our hair can do so many wonderful things and hold so many different shapes. When it comes to finding your style and taking care of your hair, learn about your hair type and texture and find the right products that work well for it. Try something new with your hair. If you get stuck in a hair rut, get inspiration from other naturals, visit a natural hair salon, try a new cut or add some color. The great thing about our hair is there are so many different possibilities when it comes to hairstyles. Have fun with it.

Be willing to adjust your self-image. Let go of how you think your hair *should* be and how your hair *should* look. We all change as we grow, and we must keep up with our ever-changing selves if we want to set and achieve meaningful goals. Wearing your natural hair takes courage and confidence and you have to be willing to stand out. Learn to walk confidently. Learning to be at peace with your self-image is one thing that you can develop when learning to love your natural hair.

Stop comparing yourself to others. Don't get hung up on someone else's style or look. Just focus on how to manipulate your hair and make it fit your style. Learn your curl pattern and texture and find a style that works for you. Reclaim your inner core of self-esteem and stop comparing yourself to other women, even the women in the natural hair community. There will be women who have beautiful curls that are always moisturized and defined or long hair that you wish you had. They seem like they have it all together, but don't compare and don't envy. That will only drag you down and make you feel insignificant. Other people are not better than you. You are who you are and there is only one you. What you bring to the world is enough and we need what you have. Comparing ourselves to others is a trap that is extremely easy to fall into, especially today with social media and the ability to project a polished, perfected appearance. The only person you should compare yourself to is you. Be whole and complete in yourself and know who you are. Don't look to social media to validate yourself. If others can't accept you, that is irrelevant.

Say "stop" to your inner critic and eliminate negative self-talk. Yes, there is such a thing as self-talk. That little voice that tells you that you're killing it (or not) is way more powerful than you might think. When I was in acting school in Hollywood, California, my instructors would always tell me to get out of my head. In other words, I had to stop thinking so much and judging my performance and instead be present in the moment. I had to train myself to stop hindering my performance because I was afraid to let go and listen to my stage partner. Just like in acting, sometimes you hear that voice that is always criticizing what you do. To begin healthy habits, you need to start talking back to the inner critic before it damages your life. Get out of your head and start living in the moment. Sometimes it's not other people who are criticizing you, only yourself. As they say, you can be your worst critic. Change how you feel about yourself by harnessing the power of your thoughts. Appreciate yourself by taking a two-minute self-appreciation break. Think about some of the things that you listed that you like about your hair and the benefits you will have when you decide to reveal your true self. Have more understanding of yourself and be kind to yourself. Write down three things in the evening that you can appreciate about yourself and speak positively about yourself.

Truly feel deserving. Stop feeling lousy about yourself and start feeling good about your hair. Believe in yourself and believe that you are somebody. Dr. Martin Luther King Jr wanted you to know that you should love who you are and not let anyone tell you that you are not worthy or fit to live in this world. Given our *hair story*, you might be dwelling in the past and on negative experiences that you've had with your natural hair that may be preventing you from having a healthy relationship with yourself. Be confident and have a positive outlook on your life. Don't focus on your weaknesses, accept them for what they are, and work on being better at taking care of your hair.

Be naturally free. There is something liberating yet strengthening about your natural hair. If you haven't done the big chop and are considering going natural, I would suggest you take the big leap. There is something spiritually cleansing and freeing when you are willing to make an extreme change and start over. It's similar to becoming a minimalist and cleaning your home from material possessions. It's like lifting a weight off of your shoulders and resetting. Also, when you do the big chop, it's easier to maintain your hair while you learn about your curl pattern and natural texture.

Express yourself. The way you wear your hair is a reflection of your opinion of yourself and your abilities. While everyone has their occasional doubts about themselves; not being able to express yourself can leave you feeling insecure and unmotivated. You might be able to identify some of the things that are affecting your opinion of yourself, like being bullied, the images you see on social media or something that is still a mystery. If you can't figure out what it is, talk to a professional or someone you trust about your feeling of inadequacy. We need to protect natural hair at all costs. Embrace everything about it; it's yours, a part of who you are.

18

TAKE UP SPACE

"Our deepest fear is not that we are inadequate. Our deepest fear is that we are powerful beyond measure. It is our light, not our darkness that most frightens us. We ask ourselves, 'Who am I to be brilliant, gorgeous, talented, fabulous? 'Actually, who are you not to be?"
- Marianne Williamson

Black women are always trying to find a seat at the proverbial table because we have been excluded for years. We are always trying to fit into someone else's box instead of stepping out and being the unique beauty that we were created to be. We complain about others not making space for us, yet we don't make space for ourselves. We're trying to stay out of the way instead of taking up space.

Black women complain about white people who appropriate black culture and complain about how white women steal our culture and make it fashionable, but no one is talking about how black women borrow from white women and how black women style their hair like white women every day. Having long and blonde straight hair is something that white women possess and black women try their hardest to look that way. You don't have to try so hard. You are beautiful with the hair you have, and you don't need to damage your hair and self-worth to feel attractive and loved. Stop putting so much time and attention into making yourself into a perfect little imitation of someone else. Be your natural self and stop apologizing for who you are. Make people make space for you and make room for your own table.

Your self-esteem is how much you value, approve, appreciate the prize, or like yourself. It is whether you are satisfied with yourself or not. It's your opinion that you hold about yourself, to determine if you are worthy. It's your value, self-respect, and self-worth. Your self-worth is an important part of why you make the decisions that you make about your hair. When you have high self-esteem, you feel positive about yourself, your actions, and your future. Too little self-esteem can leave you feeling inadequate, defeated, or depressed and can cause you to make bad choices, which ultimately lead to failing to live up to your full potential. Having a realistic and positive view of yourself is important for loving your natural self. Psychologist Abraham Maslow depicts self-esteem as one of the basic human motivations in his hierarchy of needs theory, stating that people need both self-esteem and self-respect. To grow and reach self-actualization, you need to fulfill both. You want to feel accepted, you want to feel that you have the qualities to be invited to the party, to be liked and followed. You want to feel wanted and included. Your overall sense of value or worth has been influenced by things that hurt your self-esteem, and it's time that you stop the negative talk and start moving toward valuing yourself.

You are a beautiful queen and it's time you owned your crown. For far too long, you have been deemed the outcast, the ill-favored, and the copy of someone else. You can't give the world what you have if you constantly cover it up and seek to be like someone else. Don't strive to be someone else when you can effortlessly be yourself. There is only one you, and who's better at being you than you? The world needs whatever you have to offer. We have our own rich culture and we no longer need to borrow from other women. It is nice to appreciate other people's cultures, but we have a lot to offer the world and it's time to show up and take up space.

19

THE STRENGTH OF YOUR STRANDS

Loving your natural hair will not fix all of your problems and going natural doesn't mean your life will be free of struggle, but it will help you to find the courage to stop hiding, build resilience to be unapologetically you, and make you open to being your best self. You are constantly under construction, trying to figure out your life and who you are. Just learn to let things go that are not serving you and work on giving back to yourself the things that have been torn apart by years of toxic thinking. Wearing your natural hair is not going to get rid of all of the hurt that stemmed from your past or the hurtful things that others may have said about your hair, but it is a step in the right direction. You might need to talk to a therapist about your pain because it can be that serious. After all, the hurt can cut deep. I'm not going to be dismissive of the trauma that you might have had growing up natural or returning natural, but some people are willing to help you get through the pain. I realize that it might take time because it took some time for me to get it and I still have some days where I don't feel pretty, but I repeat a positive affirmation, look at other naturals, or talk to a good friend to find the motivation to get me through. This is a constant struggle between you and the rest of the world because after you go natural, you are still going to hear the same negative things about your hair. People might treat you differently because you decided to return natural, but you have to be strong. Being natural is not for the faint-hearted. You have to be strong and you have to be brave. I know you have what it takes because you were born that way. You were born to have bold hair and you were born to wear it. You were given that hair because you are strong enough to wear it, so don't be afraid to own it.

There will be challenges when it comes to managing your natural hair but don't give up on yourself and stay strong and resilient through the tough days. There will be people who will criticize you and lash out at you for being yourself but stay level-headed to handle the negativity in an understanding way. If people are constantly giving you destructive criticism and not constructive criticism, learn to be assertive and stand up for yourself. Let people know that it is not okay to demean you and that this is your hair. You love it and you are not going to take being criticized because of it. If people don't learn to respect your decision to be yourself, then don't waste your time, spend time with people who make you happy and treat you well. When you do feel like you've failed or had a bad day, handle mistakes and failures more positively. Don't make the same mistake twice. Learn and move on. Sometimes it's hard to uncover yourself because you might find that there are things that you don't like, and it may be difficult for you to accept yourself. Eventually, you are going to have to face yourself to live out your full potential and live your best life. You deserve to live a rich and fulfilled life and you deserve to have great things. Don't go through your life hiding behind a facade of yourself. You, as a black woman, have been through too much in this country to continue to hide your natural beauty because of stipulations that have been placed on you or because it has been ingrained in you to think that you are undeserving. Take care of yourself in a way that makes you feel truly valued and find the things that you like about your hair and do the things that you enjoy. Start your journey to healing and having a healthy relationship with yourself. You can always improve yourself, no matter where you are in your natural hair journey. You can always get better at loving and appreciating yourself. Having gone through the highs and lows of natural hair myself on my natural hair rollercoaster, I find that I can be authentic and transparent with myself and others and that helps in being understood and demanding respect from others. Find your tribe. The natural hair movement is in full effect and some women are rocking their afro like a pro and those are the women you want to be around and learn from. Women who are unapologetically black. Find people who will lift you and who won't bring up negative triggers. You have been trying all your life to fit in, to be accepted, and be loved. You want to be respected and taken seriously. You want to be admired by women and wanted by men. You want to be protected and cherished and you want to be cared for and nurtured. You want all the love that you deserve from others and the one way you can get it is by trying to be like the women who are most loved, the women who are put on a pedestal and worshiped for their beauty, charisma, style, and grace. Well, black woman, you are all those things and more. You have the style, the grace, the charisma, the beauty, and you don't even have to try that hard because it comes naturally. You come from a race of kings and queens and royalty. When you let that fact sink in, then only can you realize that you are the most desired woman whom people seek to be. You are sophisticated, independent, delicate yet strong, clever, and resourceful. Throughout the years, black women have proven to be strong, independent thinkers who are innovative, creative, and trendsetters. Show that you are great and that you are grateful for what you have. Show the world that black natural hair is not a fad. This is who you are, and the natural hair movement is a movement toward self-love. You deserve the best you have to offer. You deserve to live your best life filled with love and happiness. The healing starts with you. The healing starts when you take off the mask and stop hiding. The healing starts when you stop thinking of the negative self-talk and the mark that has been placed on your black hair. You have been hurt by the things in your past and continue to suffer the abuse of people telling you that you are not good enough and that you are undeserving of love. You have to start healing by taking the time to give back to yourself. Learn how to take care of your hair with the products that work best on your natural tresses. Take the time to examine your hair and learn how to style it. Realize that you have beautiful and bountiful curls that are full and luxurious, and all they need is some tender, loving care to be happy. The problem has always been that we have been trying to hide our lovely curls by adding extensions, mounting on wigs, and adding chemicals because we never took the time to learn how to manage our hair. Don't let your hair be a mystery or a burden. Let it be an exciting journey to knowing more about yourself. Let's start setting the trends again when it comes to hair, just like in the 1970s when afros were popular and even white women *and men* wanted to have them, but this time, making it here to stay. Let's be the ones to reclaim our blackness and our culture and what makes us uniquely black. Begin your journey or get left behind. Take the necessary steps to heal from your past by taking off the things that are oppressing you and causing you to feel less than you are. You are a queen and it's time for you to rock your crown and wear your afro with pride.

The black natural hair movement has created a community that creates value for black women's self-esteem and enables us to be great. With the new natural hair movement, providing a wealth of knowledge and products, why wouldn't you want to reclaim those big beautiful locs? We have to continue to encourage each other to continue our natural hair journey and our journey back to ourselves. We should all be a part of the natural hair movement because there's strength in numbers. Black women are trendsetters. When we decide that we want to do something, we get it done.

Also, when we stick together, we can accomplish much more. The natural hair movement has evolved and gives way for the next generation to start loving whom they are and owning their natural beauty. Over the past five years, black women have been thriving due to the natural hair movement. They are freeing themselves physically and mentally from Eurocentric ideas of what they should strive to emulate. Black women are shining in their glory and it's because we've finally decided to love who we are. This is why the new natural hair movement is more than a style or a trend. It is empowering black women and the future generation to stop apologizing for who they are. It inspires them to become business owners and create jobs revolving around empowering and building black woman's self-esteem. The black natural hair movement is building a community that creates value for black women's self-worth and enables them to be awesome. When we support each other and build each other, we create a space for growth where we can flourish and thrive. In a society that restricts us from living out our full potential and sends us mixed messages about who we are and who we should be, we need to come together and show each other how we should live a life knowing our worth. When we create a safe space for each other, we create something significant. We create an incubator for the future generation to live an abundant life with no fear of living out loud. When we show up and represent, we inspire and uplift each other and let each other know that it is okay to be bold and to be yourself.

THE STRENGTH OF YOUR STRANDS

You might object to the idea of going natural and staying natural because you feel that may be too extreme, but the truth is that you are simply being yourself and if that means making some people uncomfortable, then so be it. When women during the 1970s black power movement went natural they knew that wearing their natural hair was a political statement because of the years of oppression and assimilation in the black community. They knew that if they wore their afros out, they would refuse to assimilate. They knew that their afro texture hair reflected their pride in their African ancestry. They didn't want to hide or not express themselves as black women. They knew that there was power in their hair. The longer it grows, the stronger and more confident you feel. Learning to be confident in your skin requires you to be comfortable with who you are. Look at the strength of your strands and how your hair represents power and strength. In the Bible, God gave Samson strength through his hair and when he cut it off, he lost his strength. Could it be that your hair provides strength? Well, I know that having a big head full of hair gives confidence, and wearing your afro hair is a symbol of power. Don't let anyone take away your power. There is now a new generation of millennials or whatever the experts want to label them as. There is a new generation of black girls who are growing with a wealth of knowledge of natural hair. They have more information than we had when we were growing up. If you were taught from a young age that your hair was beautiful and that there's no need to hide it, maybe you would be flaunting your natural hair. We must teach the next generation of black women to not be afraid to be themselves. We need to embolden them to take risks and defy the status quo. We need to be the example and show them that it's okay to live your life being yourself and that natural hair is beautiful. You have to walk it like you talk it. You have to live it. You have to be an example. Whether you realize it or not, the next generation wants to be like you, and they take their cues on how to navigate this life from you. Be a positive influence in someone's life and let them know that they don't have to change and that they were born enough. Don't allow your children to grow up apologizing for who they are. Let them be who they are and let them be free to be themselves. Take the time to heal so that your children aren't growing up fixing the mistakes that you've made. Show up for the next generation and show them what a real queen looks like. It wasn't until I was thirty that I finally got it. I believed what I was told until I finally stopped believing the lies. It was as simple as that. I started speaking positive things into my life about my natural self. I would begin to tell myself that I don't need to change, I don't have to live my life trying to please other people. I have amazing hair. I don't have to work so hard to fit into someone else's circle. I can create my circle and be amazing at being myself. I didn't want to waste my entire life hiding, trying to please other people to make them feel comfortable, and apologizing for being black. It took me a while to realize where the hate stemmed from, but I got it and now I'm a whole new person. It's been eight years since that argument with Dominque and since then, I've decided to start over again with the big chop. I'm still on my journey to self-discovery and transformation.

THE STRENGTH OF YOUR STRANDS

Are you ready to be free to wear your natural hair?
Are you ready to live your life being yourself?
Are you ready to start your journey?

It was a sunny day in LA when I wore my afro to a farmers' market. A man walked up to me and gave me the most inspiring compliment I had ever received in my life. He said to me, "Your hair is beautiful. It's like a gift to the world." He let me know that what I had to offer was a blessing to those around me and the fact that I chose to wear my hair and be myself added value to this world. I was able to show up that day. I'm rooting for you sis and any other natural hair queens out there flaunting her natural tresses. Are you ready to show up? Did you know that your hair is a gift to the world? Get ready to take up space, take back your power start your journey, and know that there is strength in your strands.

REFERENCES

Chapter 5
1. glamour.com. *Who Decided Black Hair Is So Offensive Anyway?* https://www.glamour.com/story/black-hair-offensive-timeline .2020
2. biography.com. *How Madam C.J. Walker Invented Her Hair Care Products* https://www.biography.com/news/madam-cj-walker-invent-hair-care-products. 2021

Chapter 7
1. nielsen.com. BLACK IMPACT: CONSUMER CATEGORIES WHERE AFRICAN AMERICANS MOVE MARKETS https://www.nielsen.com/us/en/insights/article/2018/black-impact-consumer-categories-where-african-americans-move-markets/. 2018
2. businessinsider.com. *Beauty has blown up to be a $532 billion industry — and analysts say that these 4 trends will make it even bigger* https://www.businessinsider.com/beauty-multibillion-industry-trends-future-2019-7. 2019

Chapter 8
1. The Crown Act. https://www.thecrownact.com/. 2019

2. bet.com. *A Brief History Of Black Hair Braiding And Why Our Hair Will Never Be A Pop Culture Trend* https://www.bet.com/news/features/1619/the-history-of-hair-braiding-in-black-america.html. 2019
3. Byrd, A. D., & Tharps, L. L. (2001). *Hair story: Untangling the roots of Black hair in America.* New York: St. Martin's Press.
4. glamour.com. *Who Decided Black Hair Is So Offensive Anyway?* https://www.glamour.com/story/black-hair-offensive-timeline .2020

Chapter 11

1. perception.org. THE "GOOD HAIR" STUDY RESULTS. https://perception.org/goodhair/results/. 2017

Chapter 12

1. The Crown Act. https://www.thecrownact.com. 2019

Chapter 13

1. JOSHICA BEAUTY. www.joshicabeauty.com. natural hair and skin care. 2021

Chapter 15

1. andrewalkerhair.com. Hair Typing Chart. (The Hair Type chart was created by Oprah's hairstylist Andre Walker to categorize different hair types, from straight to kinky curly. 1 being straight, 2 wavy, 3 curly, and 4 kinky curly)

I, _____ , am stepping out and taking up space. I am ready to start my journey to loving myself. I will not be afraid of _____, but I will have courage and take back my power.

What's your story? I would love to hear from you. Share your journey on Instagram and social media by tagging @thestrengthofyourstrands

www.ingramcontent.com/pod-product-compliance
Lightning Source LLC
Chambersburg PA
CBHW051450290426
44109CB00016B/1694